Twelve Promises a-Pending

How a Dozen Challenges in a Year
Transformed Our Lives

Jackie McGregor

Published in 2013 by FeedARead.com Publishing – Arts Council funded

A CIP catalogue record for this title is available from the British Library.

*To my lovely family who greet most of my
requests with smiles - I feel blessed.*

*To my pupils, past and present, who do the same – I
could not ask for more!*

Contents

Introduction

"Next!" has been the constant cry in my head from as far back as I can remember. You'd never guess from looking at me (hardly being stick thin from living on my nerves) but I'm always on the go – no, I'd better rephrase that – my brain is always on the go (my body lags at least 100 paces behind). At the moment I'm a very contented primary teacher and indeed so far in life I've been a very contented lots-of-other-things, from a video shop owner to a sign manufacturer and from a barmaid to a bookshop manager, to name a few. I seem to have found my niche with teaching but this doesn't stop me getting itchy feet. The more I encourage others to learn, the wider my own interests have become, which is saying something considering my degree encompassed studying the arts of the 18th and 19th centuries, philosophy, women's studies, criminology and the debates and practices around modern art – all ever so handy in a primary classroom I'm sure you'll agree.

I wasn't particularly academic at school and although I briefly considered teaching I was soon put off by my teacher dad who had given himself a great big 40th birthday treat by resigning from the profession. Instead I followed my dad into business and over the next 20 years I enjoyed changing my profession whenever I got an urge for a new challenge. During this time the 'study bug' also took hold and over the last 15 years I've never stopped, starting with an Open University degree and going on to a teaching career where professional development courses are an integral part of my working life.

Does it sound like I've become a wee swot? Well it's true that I've spent hours thinking about how I and others learn but if I'm honest I've spent many, many more hours poring over a Hello magazine debating whether Brad's relationship with Angelina seems more stable than his marriage to Jen (if you know what I'm talking about then you clearly have similarly, ahem, highbrow tastes!). However these vital dilemmas are not all that occupies my mind or my time and, like many of my friends I'm constantly pondering a variety of things... my relationships, my body, nail biting, exercise regime, overindulgence with sweeties and, more especially, how to change them - which brings me to this book and a scrap of an idea which began late in 2008.

Before continuing I have to look back, to give you a little insight into how our lives were in 2008 – they were complicated. Matt and I had been together since around 2004 and our lovely wee daughter Daisy was born in 2006. I had lived in the country for 20 odd years but Matt was a city boy who could no longer drive due to deteriorating eyesight, so with an incredible dearth of public transport in the country, we lived in our original own domains whilst our daughter (easily) morphed into being this little nomadic creature, living an adventurous half city/half country double life. Our lifestyle took a bit of getting used to, as did becoming a mum for the first time at 41 whilst in the middle of the most gruelling academic study I had ever encountered. It's safe to say, as with most new parents, that 2006 to 2008 went by in a bit of a blur.

In 2008 my life started returning to normal and, with studies for the moment complete, I again heard the all too familiar voice in my head whispering "Next". The thought of opening another textbook or having to

THINK too much was out of the question. I considered joining a gym but didn't want to commit for the minimum one year membership which most required. I toyed with the idea of joining a dance class or a slimming club but didn't want to commit to a weekly class. Clearly some commitment issues going on here! 'Short term' kept springing to mind and the idea for the challenges was born.

A challenge a month I decided. Could I change any of my bad habits in a month? Long enough to maybe make a change in my life but not long enough to get bored. A chance to try new things, but again, not the end of the world if I hated the process. The idea grew and grew. Maybe I could flirt with lots of different things I had never really considered seriously before. It would be like Wife Swap or Challenge Anneka – who knew what I could achieve! My main stipulation on choosing the challenges was that they wouldn't be 'easy'. They had to be real challenges to my normal behaviour or way of life otherwise there'd be no point. Lastly and on the 'not easy' note ... I was going to attempt to use the diaries I would be keeping during the challenges to write a book about our experiences ... something to leave for Daisy and ... for you, Dear Reader... and if you are out there then I have succeeded on this at least.

Matt, bless him, came on board and agreed to participate in the whole adventure. In exchange I let him have some input into what the challenges will be (how nice am I?) He also cleverly come up with a title for the book of 'Twelve Promises a Pending' believing my initial title of 'Challenging Behaviours' sounded ...... well, too boring for words.

Why, you may be asking, has such a long time passed between the original idea for this book and its final publication? We will come to that – I promise you I haven't been sitting on my big caboose, but in the interests of not putting a spoiler out there, please just trust me and being the kind of person I am ("control freak," coughs Matt) I will try to tie up loose ends (and to see just how good I am at that, please refer to February's challenge!)

Jackie McGregor
November 2013

Chapter 1 – January

Needs and not Wants

The first challenge initially sounded like a great antidote to the excesses of Christmas. We decided to call this the month of 'needs and not wants', but exactly what this would entail had to be further decided. Were we going to live this mantra to the letter? Would we exist only on water as a fluid and ration our food to the extreme of keeping us healthily alive or were we going to be a little more lax in our approach? Anyone who knows me and has observed my figure pre-and post-this experiment will realise we took the latter approach. We were extremely conscious that Daisy should not suffer in any way from our challenges – these were meant, after all, to be interesting and hopefully improve our lives in the long run - so our boundaries on this challenge were going to be buying only for 'needs' and not 'wants' as the occasion arose. We made one addendum prior to this challenge beginning – we were not allowed to stockpile goods for January but we could use any of the produce we had left in our store cupboards at the end of the year. Clearly this was not to be a challenge about living on the bare necessities, but to use imagination, creativity and any non-monetary means at our disposal to live as good a life as possible.

Thursday 1st January 2009

We ended our year yesterday with an eventful day. I think we were both subconsciously trying to 'live a little', as I, certainly, am a bit nervous about what may lie ahead this month. I expected to be sick of the excesses of Christmas so far, but possibly for the first

13

time, we had a lovely, relaxing and quiet family holiday with not so much as a hangover experienced by either of us. So yesterday we went into our favourite cafe in Edinburgh for huge bacon baguettes, took Daisy for her first cinema outing, ate a family dinner at a lovely candlelit tapas bar, went home and opened a bottle of champagne to toast the end of the old year and to await the new.

Today we stayed in Edinburgh as it's really easy to avoid spending money when most of the shops are closed. We've decided to ease ourselves into our challenge, however, by taking off to the Borders tomorrow where not only are there far fewer opportunities for spending but to actively pass a shop we would have to make a minimum 12 mile round trip.

Friday 2nd January
I know I said there were few opportunities to spend money in the Borders, but it's a 50 mile trip to get here and you pass a fabulous chippy and a hotel which does lovely bar lunches. Still feel completely in holiday mode as neither of us goes back to work till the 5th, so feel slightly deprived already – gosh, that was quick!

Sunday 4th January
Bugger. Off to visit friends for coffee and a play date for Daisy today and they've just phoned to ask us to bring them milk and bread. Awwwwwwww! – We've not spent a penny yet. Aware that this will have to change soon anyway, but holding onto my purse strings like a true Scot at the moment. When we returned home later our friends called to say they had forgotten to give us any money – bless them (they know about our challenge) but of course we (ever so lightly) said 'don't be silly'.

Spent £2.30 on bread and milk for friends – which I'm placing in the miscellaneous column of my journal as it is not one of OUR 'needs' or 'wants'. Since the spell was broken however, we also bought a litre of milk for ourselves for 51p. I hope I'm not sounding too anal about this – "Ahem," I can almost hear you answer out loud.

Monday 5th January

Back to work. Matt and I have both taken sandwiches for lunch. Loads of the staff at my school think the challenges are a great idea and much jollity was had in the staff room when I told them of several of the proposals for the year. It seems I am as far away from a money-conscious, vegetarian environmentalist as anyone can imagine (just some of the issues we have been pondering). I taught two different classes today and as we were talking about New Year resolutions I discussed some of my challenges with the pupils. I encourage them to think of their own resolutions for the year, but also wanted to show them that I am continually setting myself challenges. I have told them I will be honest with them if I fail in any of my tasks. I think they will be interested in following my progress.

I was made very aware that this challenge affects more than me however, when Daisy passed one of our regular haunts on our way home from work tonight and continually moaned, "want to go to cafe" until she finally fell asleep in the car. She did manage to briefly rouse herself to add that she also wanted to go to 'Clambers' (the soft play area we go to weekly at the Commonwealth Pool in Edinburgh). Felt it would be unfair to point out to her that you actually have to be awake to enjoy that particular activity.

15

Spent £2.88 on bread and milk, Matt £5 on lift to work.

Thursday 8th January
Surprise, surprise – started noticing some benefits from our challenge. I seem to have lots more energy even though I have not only been decorating but tonight have also cleared about a month's worth of ironing. Not sure of a reason for this excess of adrenalin – different foods, a distinct shortage of alcohol (all but one of our bottles of red wine run out on 1st January – Quelle horreur!), change of exercise (not driving at all except from Borders to Edinburgh and back), change of routine, break from the almost daily treadmill of grocery shopping or the reduction of unnecessary and usually fattening snacks and milky lattes in cafes.

Spent £2 on milk and raisin bread – trying to mix it up a little and vary breakfast and supper a little from toast and butter.

Friday 9th January
We are such lushes. A weekend without red wine started to get to us and creative thinking was brought sharply to the fore. We had smoked salmon in the freezer and some cream cheese in the fridge so called dad and asked him if he fancied some salmon mousse. "Great, thanks very much," he replied, before he had the chance to hear the second part of the proposition. "Swap you for a bottle of red wine," I said unashamedly. I had been brought up to think like a true entrepreneur from an early age. I, and many others, fondly (most people anyway!) think of my dad as a real 'Del-boy' character and from an early age my dad would take me to man (or 'child') his stall at the Sunday Ingliston market in Edinburgh. In exchange for

my help (or to give my mum a break) I was given a portion of the stall and allowed to sell my own goods. Now, when you're six or seven your 'stock' is limited, so I duly sold a proportion of my toys and games every week. I used the money I earned to buy myself new toys from other stalls. I now look back and wonder why my parents would let me sell their worked-hard-for purchases for a fraction of their value, but I'm sure they enjoyed seeing and encouraging my budding entrepreneurial spirit. They didn't even bat an eye when I sold my granddad some soldiers from a stall I'd set up in my bedroom. Quite incredible considering my granddad had bought me the soldiers in the first place!

Anyway, back to original story – the remaining 2 salmon mousses and bottle of wine were lovely, in case you were wondering.

Spent £5 for Matt's lift home from work tonight.

Sunday 11th January

Matt and I very 'fastidiously' (while semi-watching Louis Theroux's take on Asian brides) completed our list of challenges for the year. We're trying to do this as ethically as we can and are trying to avoid tasks which would be too easy over holiday periods, such as avoiding telly. However, ethics aside – I did put my foot down to vegetarianism during summer hols as I think it'd kill me to be in a Mediterranean country whilst avoiding fish and seafood. Strangely we have far too many options for challenges for the year and could, if we so desired, find enough to last at least another year. We shall see...

Monday 12th January

I've been talking about our progress in the staff room today. Some of my colleagues are thinking about setting challenges for themselves and all are dying to see the effects of the 'submissive wife' month. They asked today what month Matt gets to be a 'submissive husband' …. Dear, dear, dear – don't they know me at all, I replied – guffaws all round.

Spent £2.88 on bread and milk (yes, staple foodstuffs) and £5 on Matt's lift to work

Tuesday 13th January

Starting to get extremely twitchy and bored today. Time passes quickly when I'm working, but on the one day of the week when I am not working and Daisy is at nursery in the afternoon, I am in the routine of stopping off somewhere nice for coffee or lunch and a free read of new glossy magazines. I even started to fantasize this morning about going to Kiliminjaro cafe for a pot of tea and one of their gorgeous fruit scones. My fantasy grew at an alarming rate until I could barely focus on anything else. Ridiculous! Dropped Daisy at nursery, returned to flat and almost shouted for joy on reading a recipe for scones which did not include egg as I had none in the cupboards. Made half a dozen uninspiring scones and having sampled too many, now feel rather sick. As in most other things, fantasies should probably stay fantasies to keep the magic alive!

Spent £20 on petrol

Wednesday 14th January

Spent the morning at the museum with Daisy. Since Daisy was born this has been my favourite haunt for days out. Last autumn the majority of the museum was closed down, however, for refurbishment and for the next 2 years we are only left with the Scottish part of the museum, the science room (which is brilliant) a children's colouring area and a tiny little café. Now, since Daisy will not enter the Scottish part of the museum because it's "scary" (beautifully subdued lighting) we spent our time running between the art tables and the science museum. Each time we had to pass the café so even though I explained I had packed a picnic Daisy must have asked me 3000 times if she could have a cake. However, I asked an attendant where we could eat our snack (no food at art area) and we were directed to the only bench area I could see in the place. Within moments Daisy was munching away happily and to my delight spoke about our picnic at the museum all the way home.

On a more annoying note, I was trying to use a £1.50 voucher I had for Tesco but, after queuing for 10 minutes for the checkout, found that my shopping came to £1.46 and was told they could not accept my token even though I said I did not require change. They suggested I just pick some sweets from a nearby counter. On principle I refused and paid cash for my shopping. However, a heavy day of sandwich making for tomorrow's lunch has necessitated another trip back to same supermarket, much to my consternation. It seems we are continually being forced to over-consume without being fully aware of it. I used to be similarly annoyed as a single person by 2 for 1 offers which I would find difficult to use and would have much preferred a discount in price.

Spent £1.46 on bread, one banana and one apple, then (2nd trip) 88p on milk, then £1.88 and voucher (accepted this time) on more bread, milk and cheese (yes, 3 supermarket trips in one day – absolutely ridiculous)

Thursday 15th January

Daisy and I went to friend's house today for lunch so she could play with her little pal, Sol. My mate Morag started by saying she had nothing special in for lunch (my face fell) but quickly added that she had bought in some bacon as she thought I'd be missing my bacon rolls from the Metropole café. Bless her, bless her, bless her – I had bacon, egg and beans on rolls. Wow, just like the olden days (satisfied grin on face).

Friday 16th January

I was asked at work to pay into a kitty to buy a present for our Head Teacher's new granddaughter. Dilemma – I am good friends with my Head Teacher but this definitely is not a need. I agreed to do my own thing, knowing that, (in the event of last minute invitations to birthday parties) I had a stash of presents for children at home and if none were suitable I intended to make something (what, I don't know – I was saved from this by a lovely wee pink stuffed monkey in the prezzie box). Matt later came home to say he faced a similar dilemma at his work. It's his birthday on Sunday and traditionally in his office, whoever's birthday it is has to supply the cream cakes. Matt feels obliged to do this, but, and slightly against his will, he has agreed to take in homemade cakes to work instead. I've suggested icing them with the word 'sorry' but it doesn't look like his manly pride will let him go this far. Don't know if it's a gender difference thing but I am not at all embarrassed about being seen to struggle … or looking a fool … or not being a team player … I'll stop as I'm not sounding too good here at all.

Spent £5 on Matt's lift home from work

Saturday 17th January

We went to visit my dad's girlfriend in hospital today. We had a pack of blank notelets, which with the addition of a wee message became a get well card. I also made up a little selection of bath and beauty products, many of which originated as freebie gifts when purchasing make up and, this isn't meant in a bad way, but almost anything can look nice if care is put into the wrapping and luckily because of the time of year, we have recycled lots of lovely little bags, tissue paper and wrapping materials.

Daisy had a huge tantrum on the way home as she wanted to go to the shops. It wasn't even a very interesting shop – I had just quickly jumped out of the car to pop into the supermarket. However she obviously associates every one of our regular shopping trips with a treat of some kind, whether a comic, drink or junk. This is making us seriously think about the messages we are passing onto Daisy and have also been speaking about whether we should be including her in our challenges. So far, we think that as they are each only for one month, then as long as we put in plenty of effort in making sure she is not physically or emotionally deprived in any way, then ultimately we are hoping we are changing our lives for the better and will take the decision on whether to include her in each challenge one step at a time. Plus, anyone who knows our babe can clearly see that not attending purely to wants should do her no harm at all. It reminds me of my mum's memories that as a chubby 5 year old I used to stand in the bakers asking for cream cakes and moaning that I, "was starving", whilst the ladies behind the counter tried desperately to keep a straight face. Having said that, I am aware that Daisy's feeling of deprivation just now is real – why else would I have spent the last 2 minutes staring at a half-price packet of hot cross buns in the supermarket trying to justify if I should buy them (I didn't) when I don't even like hot-cross buns that much.

I babysat at night for my friends Seonaid and George. Whilst writing this diary I rather guiltily tucked into their shortbread and biscuits. Scratch the deprivation comments from above.

We spent £5.31 on eggs, bread, cheese and mushrooms ('A necessity?' I hear you ask. I agree, but something was needed to go with the present of fillet steaks my dad has bought for Matt's birthday tomorrow and although Matt is completely behind these challenges, it was my idea in the first place and he had just treated me to the most wonderful birthday in December ... guilty justifications over, OK?)

Sunday 18th January

Matt's birthday. Seonaid babysat Daisy till after lunch and Matt and I relaxed and ate lovely risotto from store cupboard ingredients and drank the bottle of champagne we were given at Christmas. At night I cooked the fillet steak from dad – yum, what a treat. Yippee – we now have an abundance of red wine in the house again as half a dozen friends and family gave Matt wine or choccies for his birthday. Looks like our ever-lessening trips to the glass recycling bins will soon increase again.

Monday 19th January

Spent £5 Matt's travel to work, £1.53 milk

Tuesday 20th January

Spent £2.33 on onions, butter and mushrooms, then 86p on milk

Wednesday 21st January

Getting really fed up now. My friend Carol asked if Daisy and I wanted to meet her at the Gyle shopping centre for lunch. She offered to treat us. I had to refuse as we are not in the habit of buying each other lunch. Starting to realise how little we are seeing of some of our friends this month. We've not met up at all with our friends who we meet weekly at the soft play.

I've been looking at the list of supplies we have bought so far this month and can see how little fresh produce we have bought. Our store cupboards are now almost empty of dried fruits and juices so we're going to have to increase our intake of frozen veggies to try to get anywhere remotely near our 5 a day (not that I think we did this often before the challenge started).

Spent £3.25 on bread, cherries and (needed but not wanted) sanitary products.

Thursday 22nd January

Daisy and I started off the day back at the museum. She did not ask for anything in the café once but immediately ran to 'her' bench for a picnic snack. It makes me realise how quickly I could break her of any bad habits we have helped her to acquire if I really tried. We then went on to have lunch again with Morag and Sol. They had invited us to join them with friends at a shop where children can paint pottery as the adults get a chance to gab. I had to decline unfortunately but eagerly accepted lunch invitation. Lovely repeat of last lunch we had there – bacon, egg, sausage and beans on rolls followed by yogurts, smoothies and chocolate for Daisy. She tucked in like a little horse, bless her. It is not that she has been deprived of quantities of food at all but she definitely enjoys the return of some of her old favourites. Again feel slightly guilty that we are including her in this part of the challenge but I am also becoming more and more aware that plenty of people are living like this all the time.

Yesterday I had met an old lady outside Daisy's nursery who asked if I wanted a £4 voucher for Sainsbury's. I replied that that was very kind of her and said I would spend it on treats for the nursery. She then asked for the £4. I was completely taken aback as this well-spoken, smartly-dressed woman was far, far away from my imagined vision of 'needy'. What assumptions we make! I explained I did not have cash on me but I spent a long time after thinking about the hardships many people are facing today.

Our lives are more uncertain in the current economic climate than they have been for some time. The credit crunch is truly biting and many previously safe jobs are on dodgy ground. This challenge is actually bringing Matt and I closer. We are talking about the way we spend money and are jointly thinking of ways to make life as enjoyable as possible on a budget, particularly for Daisy. We constantly talk about the things we take for granted. In Matt's case this was highlighted today by not being able to buy a cup of coffee at the train station whilst waiting for ages for a train. He spent this time productively however – by fantasizing about the sandwiches and biscuits he might get at his meeting (he didn't get biscuits).

Friday 23rd January
At school I was telling the pupils in my class that I had been buying things for the nursery for Chinese New Year, when one of them piped up, "That's not really a need, Miss McGregor". How right she was, but I explained that I had been given the money by the

nursery for the goods. "Before or after?" another continued to question me. How glad I was that I had been given the money beforehand, with an inquisition team like that setting upon me! I'm actually dead chuffed that my pupils are taking such an interest and are thinking about what we all actually need in life. I have looked at this subject before with pupils and it is amazing how many of them have considered telly, computer games and sweets 'needs'. The fact that my pupils are 'living' this experiment with me makes it real for them and is encouraging their learning along with ours. Getting a real buzz from this – this is what teaching should be all about.

We spent £20 petrol, £5 on Matt's lift from work and £5.03 on milk, bread, orange juice and hot cross buns – I know, I know, I didn't buy them last week but I'm justifying that we will use them for breakfasts on Saturday and Sunday and they were only 50p and they are a change from bread and they may not be a desperate need but then neither is bread, so I'm considering buying breakfast a 'need' and this is what I am choosing to constitute breakfast – OK?

Sunday 25th January

We had visited my dad's girlfriend yesterday as she's now out of hospital so we made her a few fairy cakes with the remaining egg we had in the house. Today we were to go back for Sunday dinner and having been taught never to go empty handed a bit of quick thinking was needed. Oh the shame of it – we had bought an expensive packet on lemon bon bons last month and had opened them. We didn't like them, so today I very carefully sealed the packet and took them as a present. I also took a bottle of mulled wine syrup which was 26 days out of date but at least had the grace to explain this. The shame, the shame!

We spent £1.96 on milk and rolls

Monday 26th January
We spent £5 on travel for Matt and £2.86 on milk and bread

Tuesday 27th January
We spent £4.05 on bread, butter, onions, carrots and apples

Wednesday 28th January
My watch stopped working today. Is a new battery a 'need' or a 'want' whilst I still have a mobile phone which displays the time? I figure if I was going to be doing this challenge for another month I would renew the battery therefore I probably should do so now. I am starting to become quite fanatical or obsessive about my decision making. My addictive personality is definitely coming to the fore.

Late at night Matt and I relaxed into bed. "3 days to go," I sighed. "I can't believe you're counting down so much," said Matt, "I'm finding there's something almost spiritual…" he began, before we both began hooting with laughter. Bollocks! We both want steak, lattes and treats.

We spent £2.88 on bread and milk

Thursday 29th January
Morag and Sol are coming for a lunch (of macaroni) today. I bought brioche for an after lunch treat for Daisy and Sol and in trying to justify this extravagance, I plan to substitute the remainder for bread in our

breakfasts over the next day or two (shades of 'the lady doth protest too much'???).

Sol is about to start at the same nursery as Daisy so Morag and I have already been plotting afternoons out together with lovely lunches. Morag was asking what great plans Matt and I have for February but the truth is that although a latte in a café is top of my agenda, we have little desire to 'blow' money which we have taken so much care over saving so far. At the moment I'd love to see if we can continue saving after this challenge is over and ideally, would like to try living on Matt's wage alone for as long as possible. This challenge has shown us that this should be an attainable goal. I'm feeling a great deal of satisfaction at having achieved our January goal. This is making me more and more ambitious. I'd love to think that all things are possible – perhaps a bigger flat next year is a realistic goal.

We spent £4 on milk, cheese and brioche

Friday 30th January
We spent £5 on travel for Matt and £4.29 on bacon and bread

Saturday 31st January
I would have loved to have ended this chapter on the wonderfully positive note from yesterday but today has felt completely different. We have a friend, Gail, staying tonight. She brought down loads of wine and we made a nice risotto dinner. There was, however, no pudding, no decent coffee, no snacks and the toilet roll situation is becoming worryingly low. So, I am feeling a lack of 'stuff', am missing 'stuff' and am generally in a really crabby mood. Roll on tomorrow!

THE SPEND IN JANUARY

For those of you who are as 'picky' as I am (there's a nicer word than I usually use) I have tried to detail my spending as I went along. So ...

The big summary is as follows – da da da da da da (fanfare !!??!!)

Total spent on food, toiletries etc £46.52 (IN THE WHOLE OF JANUARY –

Can you believe it?)

Total spent on travel £80 (£40 petrol and £40 lifts for Matt)

Total spent on miscellaneous £2.30 (the bread and milk for friends at the start of the month – not that they should feel guilty – even seeing this in print).

GRAND TOTAL   £128.82

I can safely say this has all been spent on 'needs' and not 'wants', though the brioche and hot cross buns have taken some explaining and are still acting as a bit of a thorn in my usually honest conscience.

Afternote

On the 1st of February we went to a local garden centre for lunch. We ordered a toastie, panini, 2 lattes, apple juice and 2 tray bakes. The bill was £15.35, the equivalent to 2 weeks previous food bill. We felt so naughty we sat and giggled like little kids, but, boy, was it good!

We then went to the supermarket to do a 'big shop'. We bought less, in fact, than in our old supermarket spending sprees. We stocked up heavily on fresh produce and replenished our stores of dried and frozen fruits and vegetables. Although neither Matt or I are huge vegetable eaters (or indeed thought we were not) we have noticed that this month the condition of our skin and hair was not as good as usual and we can only put this down to a lack of fresh produce, as we have been eating a less balanced diet than usual. We made an effort to ensure Daisy ate fruit, vegetables or drank whole fruit juices every day but in doing so limited our own consumption. However, on a positive note, if our appearance seems less than wholesome, we have the whole of next month to more than make up for it.

Chapter 2 – February

Attention to Detail

Our February challenge was initially suggested by Matt. As a Chartered Quantity Surveyor he has spent most of his professional life out on mucky building sites. In the past year, however, he had been employed by a city firm and as he is now predominantly office based he feels that his image needs somewhat of an overhaul. True, he goes to work every day in a suit and tie and in autumn and winter adds a long black wool coat to his ensemble, but, much as I love Matt to bits, no one could accuse him of paying attention to detail. It is hard to know whether a touch of 'sloppiness' is simply a character trait akin to his partner's or if it can be put down to his eyesight, as he is partially sighted. However, on a daily basis, Matt asks me to pick out the closest-to-white shirt I can find and he has a feeling that this is clearly flagging up an area he needs to concentrate on.

I am certainly not naturally a smart or tidy person. 'Relaxed', 'informal' or on a rare, good day, 'funky' are adjectives which would be most accurate in describing my sense of dress. I sometimes fear 'midden', 'scabby' or 'tramp' are more often uttered when I am out of earshot. However, I would have to say that I am approaching this challenge with a heavy heart. I think I might find it too shallow. I personally find people who are too smartly dressed unnerving and secretly believe they must have too little of any importance going on in their lives. But …. I have to support Matt … Perhaps my self esteem might hugely benefit from all the compliments I may receive and what the hell, could looking tidy FOR A MONTH REALLY BE THAT BAD?

Sunday 1st February

Well, the answer to the previous question is 'yes!' We both hated to get up to iron clothes in order to go for a casual coffee to the garden centre. Matt duly ironed and put on his shirt and a button immediately fell off. He went out without sewing it on, the slut (or the male equivalent thereof)! But, be assured, I'll make him sew it on tonight – this challenge being his idea and all.

As a little aside from my own point of view, it was rather nice to bump into my old university tutor when I looked presentable. In the evening though, I had to throw all my clothes in the wash when I would have sneaked an extra day's wear out of the lovely skirt I had only had on for a few hours. A waste of environmental resources I'd say.

Tues 3rd and Wed 4th February

Went on a shopping spree today, hoping to pick up some nice new clothes. Instead I bought clothes for Daisy and Matt. For myself I found a top in a sale for £15 and renewed some of my underwear. I'm not exactly excited about this, it doesn't help my outward appearance, but at least if my bra strap is showing it will be white and not the usual charming grey hue. Slightly more conscious than usual of what I was buying, I also bought matching pants for about the first time ever. Not painting a lovely picture of my usual self, am I?

Tues 10th February

Matt's turn to go on a spending spree. He was a little more successful than I was. He bought 7 shirts, the

31

most expensive being a pink dress shirt which he was very happy with till I conveyed my surprise at him choosing pink. "Pink?" he responded and the shirt is now getting taken back to the store. I keep trying to get Matt to buy more 'European'-style or at least, adventurous clothes, but the building trade side of him (with the implicit danger of getting a very hard time for being a wuss) usually kicks in quite swiftly.

Wednesday 11th February

How exciting my life has become with this challenge. I de-bobbled a jacket and rubbed lint off a pair of cords whilst watching telly. I moaned to Matt at night about how bored I am. He suggests looking at this long term and said that although he is making tiny and unnoticeable changes just now he is hoping that these small changes will alter his ways of thinking about appearance in the long run. I'm certainly noticing how much smarter Matt looks in his new shirts and for £6.50 a piece this is quite impressive.

Friday 13th February to Sunday 15th February

The three of us have come on holiday to Crieff Hydro for two nights for a bit of pampering and, wait for it, 6 hours of 'free' childcare per day. Realise Matt is right (who said that?) and that this challenge is a process which is starting this month. I've been spending all my spare time in the child free Victorian spa, lying in the jacuzzi, steam room or on a lounger, reading, resting or deep in contemplation (i.e. sleeping whilst trying hard not to snore). I am enjoying this 'me' time so much that I am toying with joining a health spa. I am also conscious that to look my best I must not only concentrate on my outer appearance but must make an effort to get my body into better shape. I have been overweight for many years and although I occasionally try to diet (and am successful during the period I diet) my weight invariably creeps back up when I resume my old eating patterns – no surprise. I know the likes of Oprah talk about weight control patterns being symptomatic of deeper issues but I really believe it is because I simply like food and eat too much rather than any deep seated issue. I also know that I am not any happier when at a lighter weight with the exception of having a greater choice of clothes in the shops. However, I am ready to try something new and the one thing I have not attempted in taking care of myself is exercise, so upon returning home I am going to contact some gyms to investigate my options. As with this whole experiment, I would like to try to enjoy the PROCESS of change rather than simply be concerned with the RESULT.

Friday 20th February

And ... RESULT! – Have had a whole day of positive comments on my appearance. Went into work wearing a new jumper I bought in Crieff (I also had a big spend earlier in the week at Ragamuffin, my favourite shop in Edinburgh). I had also been using a moisturiser which contains fake tan, still had on the false nails I had applied at Crieff and was wearing a beautiful new lipstick which is meant to last all day (it did). I certainly must have looked different to my usual school self because almost every member of staff commented on my appearance. The same thing happened at my book club in the evening and so, I'd have to say, I've felt really good all day. We'll have to see if it's enough to keep me inspired to maintain the effort.

Saturday 28th February

Jings– I've just re-read the previous entry and have to contend with the fact that the compliments were NOT enough to help me maintain the effort. The lack of diary entries may be a clue, but, I'd have to say our responses to this month's challenge have been a resounding FAILURE. Matt says that he has been thinking about his appearance for the first time in many years ("thinking" – good effort Matt!) and is convinced he will pay more attention in the future. I am not. I still believe life's too short and although I enjoyed receiving compliments they did not mean enough to me to make these changes long-lasting. I'd prefer my actions or the way I live my life to be considered rather than simply my outward appearance. Would I think any differently if I looked like Heidi Klum – next life perhaps! As for joining a gym – I managed to stay resolute on that option for almost a week!

Chapter 3 – March

10,000 Steps a Day

The idea for this challenge was originally conceived when I read that the government's guidelines for a healthy active life was to aim for 10, 000 steps a day and like most people I have spoken to about this, I had no idea what these figures meant in reality. Our timing for this challenge did not seem ideal as we had only just finished thinking about our appearance, but we quickly realised that this would be a completely different type of challenge – we were not doing this predominantly to change our appearance but to benefit our health. The failure of last month's challenge has had an effect on me, however, and I have decided to combine the walking with some very sensible eating. I just read an interview with Steven Fry and when he was asked how he had lost weight he replied, "Astonishingly, I ate less food!" Sometimes things just seem so bloody obvious that you are surprised you had not thought of them earlier and so instead of joining a gym I am going to dedicate a month to eating less food and getting off my butt a bit more often.

Sunday 1st March
I'm psyched! We're both extremely enthusiastic about starting this challenge and although Matt and I woke up this morning with the start of a cold, sore throat and bunged up noses, we have put on our comfy shoes and set out in the glorious (for March) sunshine for a walk with Daisy. Realising the fickle nature of a 2 year old and having no idea of how far we would cover we took the buggy. Good job we did too! It took us an hour and

a half to cover 5, 000 steps but in which time we wandered round Kelso Abbey, fed the ducks, looked at the river and generally had a lovely family day out. By the end of the day we had both completed our 10, 000 steps but I'm slightly worried about how I will fit in time to do this during a school day.

Monday 2nd March

Re yesterday's worries – no problem at all! By the end of the school day I had completed 8, 000 steps which amazes me. I knew teaching a P1-3 class often left me exhausted by the end of the day but I thought it was from the constant attention and sitting down and standing up all day – I had no idea I actually moved around so much. Matt has similarly found that between his normal work routine, walking to work and back and collecting Daisy from nursery he has totalled 7, 000 steps before he comes home. Is this going to make the challenge too easy? Should we increase our limit? At the moment I think we have to stick to original challenge until we see how things go.

On a slightly more worrying note I weighed myself and took my measurements today. There's no way I'm going to write down what they are but I will monitor them again at the end of the month and will report back on how they have changed (positive thinking).

Tuesday 3rd March

Eureka! I've rushed home after dropping Daisy at nursery to make this diary entry. It is only just after 1pm and I have already done over my 10, 000 steps for the day. Between walking to the shops, meeting a friend for coffee and taking Daisy to nursery the steps have been whizzing by on the pedometer. My feet are aching but I have deliberately left the buggy at nursery so that I have to walk there to collect Daisy tonight, ensuring another hour's walk. I'm so excited to be enjoying this challenge that I'm only slightly upset that the cheapo pedometers I bought are constantly falling off both Matt and I and are constantly resetting, so, dear reader, I may have now covered 100, 000 steps – though I seriously, seriously doubt it.

One thing I did want to add is that our previous challenges seem to be coming together. The friend I met for coffee recommended I order freshly brewed coffee at Starbucks rather than my usual latte or Americano and I discovered that not only is it much cheaper but you are entitled to a free refill. I'll be back. Often! Alongside this, during my walk today I started musing on the fact that I had put on fake tan this morning and spent a bit of time on my makeup, probably because I didn't have to, so there seems to be a kind of synchronicity emerging, don't you think?

Added in evening

I'm very, very tired and will definitely be in my bed by 9.30pm as I have walked 20, 000 steps today. Yippee!

Wednesday 4th March

In contrast to what I wrote earlier in the month about not dieting (and not at all like my usual fickle self) I have decided to try to count calories some of the time. I figure if I stick to about 1500 a day on the days we are not socializing then I should be able to splurge a bit every few days. I'm astonished at how little food this allows on days I'm being careful. No wonder I've constantly added half a stone a year over the last few years – I eat a LOT. I'm still feeling really positive about this challenge. Today I made a conscious effort to take Daisy out in the buggy for a long walk then we went to the museum so she could run around and blow off steam for ages. Between this and walking to the cinema and back when she was at nursery (where I collapsed in front of the film 'The Class' with a coffee and a packet of chocolate covered raisin Poppets for only 149 kcals) I have managed today to again take a total of 20, 000 steps. Not only that but, wait for it, I did 10 sit ups and 10 kind-of- pretend press ups (on my knees). To illustrate my fastidiousness, before starting I even phoned a friend to ask if she could do any real press ups, as I was slightly worried that my upper arms were made of foam instead of muscle. She, though slim is as equally exercise obsessed as myself and quickly assured me that only super-athletic women would even attempt such a thing. Well now you realise not only why I have such a good relationship with my pals but also may detect some ever so slightly obsessive behaviour patterns emerging. I would now keep obsessively typing but it's 9.40pm and I need to use my last available burst of energy to clean my teeth and go to bed. Good night. zzzzzzzzz

Thursday 5th March
Took my pedometer back to the chemist I bought it at today. By the end of the school day it said I had done almost 19, 000 steps and there's no way I have done that. True, I was tired but our school is not huge and I didn't spend my breaks walking at breakneck speed to I can safely say it must be broken. I am desperately hoping it has just broken now and has not been miscounting over the last few days. I'm pretty sure I have completed 20, 000 for the last couple of days however as I have spent many hours walking around town. The chemist won't have any more in stock till Tuesday so I'm going to try to buy a new one in

Edinburgh at the weekend. For the moment I'll just have to keep as active as possible.

As an additional note, the staffroom today was filled with rather unusual activity. I asked the PE teacher to show me how to correctly do a press up. She showed me how to initially start and then add to the level of difficulty as I become fitter. Glad no parents walked in! I am continuing with sit ups and press ups in the evening.

Matt has not fared too well either with his pedometer. He has dropped it so many times that it is now furiously flashing away but refusing to count – as obstinate as its owner it seems, so looks like all the money we saved in January may have to go towards financing our pedometer habit.

Monday 9th March

Oh oh – I'm in trouble! I bought a new super-duper fancy pedometer yesterday - £25 as opposed to £3.99 and spent ages last night adjusting the settings to my weight, step stride, etc. Before buying it I did my research on the computer. Apparently it calculates steps by three different measurements and does not miscount steps which are shuffles, individual or small patterns of steps or movement such as jumps and in fact only begins to calculate steps when you have been walking properly for 7 continuous seconds (otherwise it would claim, if it could speak, that you were not in fact 'walking' but simply 'moving'). 'Sounds brilliant', I thought, only ….. Today I've only done 3679 bloody steps plus a tremendous amount of shuffling (note to self – pick up feet!). I am, as you can imagine, impressed with the technology but totally bloody sick with how inactive it makes me sound.

Tomorrow I will make up for today's lost steps and as for the previous 8 days ... I stand by the pedometer readings I have received thus far (note how I stray into persuasive almost biblical or legal jargon when I'm trying to justify my actions). I'm afraid I may prefer to live in oblivion to here!

Wednesday 11th March

I am absolutely physically shattered and for the second night in a row I am going to bed very, very early and expect to flake out the second my head hits the pillow. My legs are aching, my feet are throbbing, I am struggling with my sit ups and despite my best efforts I have still not been able to make up for Monday's deficit over the last couple of days. I managed just over 11, 000 on Tuesday and have done my 10, 000 today and I am now in no doubt that I preferred my old pedometers. I do know, however, that my new pedometer is actually measuring my exercise – after all, how could a few steps within my classroom or around my kitchen when preparing dinner be considered exercise? There is one thing that this super duper pedometer does not take into account however – I spent half an hour at Clambers, the soft play place yesterday with Daisy and hardly stopped the whole time I was there, but because I was climbing or jumping around rather than walking it did not register at all on the pedometer and was not included in my total calories burnt. Leading on from this thought, today Matt brought home a box of Hotel Chocolat chocolates he had ordered for me. Normally I would have used this as the perfect excuse to get tucked in, but, just as I resisted any snacks at the cinema this afternoon, I am being on my best behaviour. Old habits die hard and despite trying not to 'diet' I cannot wait to weigh or measure myself – I won't though as it would kill me if I feel this sore and had not lost any weight or worse still, put weight on.

A note on how Matt is doing with this challenge - Well, in addition to breaking his original pedometer he seems to forget to wear his current 'cheapie' pedometer every day. Yesterday he suggested he was going to buy a new, better one but I, rather forcefully suggested he tries remembering to wear his existing one first (I must assert myself before next month – but more of that later). He thinks he covers most of his walking on his journeys to and from work but is not 'pacing the room' in the evening to make up the extra steps required. He has been fastidiously doing his sit ups (15) and press ups (10) at the same time as me, though as I have been toying with the idea of stopping the sit ups as they're hurting my back (I know I'm probably not doing them properly). I haven't told him yet but I've ordered an exercise DVD from Amazon with short 10 minute exercise routines for toning stomach, bum, arms and legs. This I either plan to use or add to my existing pile of unwatched exercise DVDs at home.

Thursday 12th March

I've just got into school and have already eaten my lunch and it's not even 9am yet. True, my lunch rarely lasts untouched until lunchtime and most often gets nibbled by break time, but this shows a particularly strong lack of restraint even for me. Having said that, I didn't have time for breakfast this morning – it's particularly hard getting out the door for seven o'clock when Daisy is mucking about playing with hair bands, toying with her toast, trying to find her favourite dollies and her pink wig so that she looks like Stephanie out of Lazytown. Nevertheless I am convinced the additional exercise I am doing is raising my appetite. My plan for today is to spend the first half hour of my lunchtime walking round the village or around the large grassy field beside our school in order to have a chance to make up the deficit in steps this week (still have an extra 4, 000 to make up).

Added later. I've just managed to complete my day on 11, 000 steps. In order to achieve this I had to walk for three quarters of my lunch break and take a walk after school. By late evening I had reached my 10, 000 steps but instead of sitting on my bottom watching telly I walked around my living room while watching telly, puffing and panting all the way. I'm feeling dead proud of myself and extremely enthusiastic about this project. I think I'd like to incorporate this into my life all the time, especially if it means I can eat more without having to think about dieting.

Friday 13th March

Just got into school and told a colleague about my striding around the living room. She asked why I didn't march in one place so I could see the telly better. Twit that I am, I had never considered it and I've just tried it – it works.

Matt and I went out for a meal at our friends, Myra and John's house tonight. After trying to stick to around 1500 calories a day I felt completely stuffed before the sweet had even arrived. However I forced myself to have some as it was Myra's fabulous chocolate tart. Feel utterly spoiled but gained back some self control by driving there and back so cutting out the calories from alcohol at least.

My walking fared slightly worse today - despite spending some of my lunch hour and some time after school walking, I have only managed to do 6, 000 steps and am now 7, 000 down on the week. I'll have to make real efforts this weekend to make it up.

Sunday 15th March

By walking in front of the telly last night for over an hour I managed to claw back 1, 000 steps, but despite my best efforts I still haven't managed to claw back the deficit today. Daisy got me up at 6.30 this morning and I immediately got up and started moving. I left Matt in bed and set off for Kelso to go to the market, car boot sale and the garden centre, but as nothing had really started by the time we got in we went to the supermarket to buy bread and went to feed the ducks instead. Daisy is getting pretty heavy to push now in the buggy and by eleven o'clock and 6, 000 steps later I was absolutely shattered and had to go for a wee sleep when I got home. When I was walking in Kelso I held my pedometer and was extremely disappointed to see it was failing to register about a third of my steps. I told Matt when I got home and he said it was probably just not getting a big enough 'jog' in my hand (very scientific explanation) and probably worked fine (as it is meant to) in my pocket. In the afternoon, to give me more energy I had to eat 800 calories worth of Hotel Chocolat chocolates – the things I do for my sport!

Matt has forgotten to bring his pedometer to the cottage. I very much doubt he managed his steps today, unless he did them in dreamland of course. He keeps telling me he does at least that amount of steps by walking to work and when he is out on site in his job, so his plan is to instead follow an exercise routine. He borrowed a marines' fitness book from his brother Tom, but it seems to be staying very inert on our shelves. Our fitness DVD arrived from Amazon on Friday so after our lovely steak dinner we sat in our

43

comfy chairs and watched the thigh toning section. It looks good. We may even do it one day. Daisy asked for her 'training shoes' on and bounced around in front of the telly. Very funny. Worth it just for that!

Monday 16th March

A real low day as far as exercise goes. Even though I worked non-stop all day at school, rushed to a professional development meeting 20 miles away then drove 50 miles to get home, completely exhausted, I have only managed 4, 000 steps today. Off to bed now, extremely early, and will try to catch up on my days off.

Thursday 19th March

As if I was not tired enough this week (I can proudly state I made great strides on managing to catch up on a 9, 000 step deficit and am now only 3, 500 down), I had to go to work today on about 2 hours sleep. Matt was dealt a body blow yesterday – either work for the majority of the week in Wales or face possible or probable redundancy. We talked all night, then fought, cried and finally managed to hold a reasonably sensible discussion. I'm against him going. It's incredibly important to me that Daisy has as stable a life as possible, especially with so many 'unknowns' in our lives. At the moment we're on the move all the time, we work 50 miles apart from each other, Daisy has two sets of friends and two nurseries depending on when I'm working and …. Aaaaagh! …. Sometimes it is just so complicated it's unreal. On the flip side of the coin though, Matt is incredibly worried that in this economic climate he will not be able to find another job. It took him a year and a half to get the job he's in – most companies seemed to shy away from employing a disabled person and some made it more explicit than others in their explanations. As I type this I'm still in such a quandary – Matt wants desperately to provide for his family and I want him to have a stable family to provide for. I'd also be fine with being the breadwinner if that would help. Shit! Shit! Shit! At least one thing's helping a bit – we lived on very, very little in January. I hope it wasn't a dry run for things to come, but, if the circumstances dictate that then at least we know we can live a LOT more frugally.

Sunday 22nd March

Help! I'm starting to panic. I've been slightly overdoing the celebrations for Mother's Day i.e. I started celebrating on Friday and have not yet stopped. I have eaten a million calories each day and have taken on a strange sloth-like appearance. On Friday I managed only 6, 000 steps, on Saturday 4, 000 and today again a paltry 4, 000. I am now a total of 22, 000 down which seems like a rather large mountain to climb before the end of the month. Still, I am bloody determined – I am going to do it. Watch my dust (Not just now you understand – there won't be much dust as I meander through to bed to watch yet another DVD) !

P.S. On Saturday I went to a teaching function at the Scottish Parliament. As we parked up Daisy asked if we could climb the big mountain (Arthur's Seat – a big hill, not really a mountain). Ashamed to say I was glad I could get out of it. Matt went half way up before Daisy fell asleep in the buggy and he could slink back down again to a café. It's sometimes hard to tell which of us is the least energetic.

Thursday 26th March

Dead proud of myself – I've managed to make up lots of the deficit this week and am currently only 9, 000 steps down. As I now only have a few days till I weigh myself and take my measurements I have upped the pace for my exercising and now do 20 sit ups and 20 push ups a night. I know this is still really measly compared with people who regularly exercise, but, I only ever intended to better my own fitness not compete with others - having said that, I stopped counting calories when I was out with a friend yesterday afternoon as we sat over a yummy and rather boozy lunch.

In order to increase my steps on my work days, I either walk away from the school, or, if the weather looks bad, around the playground. As the children are not allowed out of view of the playground supervisor they now walk with me for half my journey then lie in wait, cheering me on, as I puff my way round the second semi-circle. It's actually lovely and heart warming that they are so interested. I'm not quite sure how I explain April's 'submissive wife' challenge to a primary school-aged audience though!

Monday 30th March

I did not manage to make up the extra steps I needed on either Friday or Saturday and woke on Sunday with a massive task hanging over me. Still, I am absolutely determined I will pass this challenge so I not only walked for miles yesterday but also spent ages marching in front of the telly at night. In total I did 17, 500 steps and am now only 5, 000 down in total. I'm optimistic.

I've not been weighing or measuring myself but yesterday I tried on a pair of trousers which have been too tight for over a year and they fit perfectly. What a feeling! I've always claimed being overweight was not a major problem for me, but boy oh boy, did I feel great in my purple trousers. I'm looking forward to weighing and measuring myself on Wednesday morning and although I do not want to become a slave to the scales, I hope they show a significant loss. I know as well as almost any other woman how ridiculous our relationships with the scales can be. Although we all know how our body weight can fluctuate, it can ruin your day when you've been watching what you eat and yet can put on a pound or two. I should be content with being able to fit into my purple trousers, but I don't think I'm yet that evolved.

Tuesday 31st March
Finished. Made it – 10, 000 steps a day for a month plus my added sit-ups and press-ups (now 20 of each). Shattered. What a bad attitude. So, so tired I'm even looking forward to being a submissive wife.

Postscript
I've got absolutely no intention of telling anyone my weight, either before or after, but here are the results after one month of effort:
  Lost 10.2 lbs
  BMI (Body Mass Index) down almost 2%
  Inches lost from bust – 0
  Inches lost from waist – 1
  Inches lost from hips – 1
  Inches lost from EACH thigh – 1.5
  I've got to admit, when I first stood on the scales and measured myself I was disappointed that I had not lost more, but when I think about it I was not exactly dieting and was never hungry. I occasionally wanted a bacon

roll, latte or bar of chocolate, but I did not exactly restrict myself. Apart from eating a huge box of chocolates and having 2 huge bacon baguettes at my favourite café, it seems through looking back at my diary for the month that I also managed to have 2 dinner parties, went out for meals twice and met up with friends for lunch five times – not too shabby! Even if I don't keep up with the walking I think I can maintain this lifestyle.

Chapter 4 – April

Submissive Wife/Dominant Husband

The reactions we have received to this month's challenge have been, in the main, mixed according to gender. Men have usually greeted the premise by exclaiming to Matt, "Lucky b*****d!" whereas my women friends have either hooted with laughter, loudly exclaimed "You've no chance!" or pleaded to be invited for dinner this month as a chance to witness this spectacle for real. I must say I feel equally incredulous that this challenge stands a chance of success.

The whole idea of this challenge is NOT so that Matt can fulfil all his secret, hidden sexual fantasies. It was, as with the other challenges, a chance for both of us to take on roles unfamiliar to ourselves. Many people have asked when it's Matt's turn to take on the role of submissive husband, but if you've got a similar query please simply re-read the previous sentence!!!

I hate the idea of having to ask permission from a man or to think of my role as catering to his needs, but to help me think about the issues which may arise I ordered a book from Amazon about being a 'surrendered wife' and this claims to be written by a feminist who says you can improve your partnership by surrendering yourself to your spouse. 'How rigid should the terms be?' is one of the questions we asked ourselves. Do I have to ask Matt's permission to go out or spend money? Should I make sure the house is sparkling, his shirts are ironed and there a lovely meal on the table every night? Does Matt have to order for me in restaurants? If Matt always has to take the dominant role in the bedroom (and I am not completely opposed to this concept 'in theory' or rather 'in fantasy') then how does he know if I am doing things solely to please him or when I can't be bothered, making him feel like a complete cad? Similarly Matt must worry that any of his actions or inactions will result in a complete freeze of affection come May. At the moment neither of us knows how this month will go although we both suspect there may be rocky times ahead.

Wednesday 1st April

Today is Daisy's 3rd birthday so I awoke with great excitement for the day ahead – nothing to do with this challenge you understand! I had a lovely morning with Daisy and when she went off to nursery I raced around the supermarket taking the opportunity to buy Easter eggs whilst out of her sight. My caring for my family further extended to buying my wonderful spouse an Easter egg to nibble on over the next couple of nights as he has a particularly sweet tooth. Thinking of my partner, caring, generous – am I not the picture of a dedicated wifely-person?

Postscript
Matt took advantage of his role as dominant spouse late last night – rarely before has he heard the words "whatever you want".

Thursday 2nd April

Grrrrrrrrrrrr! Yesterday's good mood did not last long. I left the house this morning in such a temper. Here's my list:

- Matt had soaked the bathroom floor (not noticed till much later) when bathing Daisy. She was playing with her new birthday bath dolly. When Dolly has a bath she gets filled with water then OBVIOUSLY you must empty it before taking it out of bath – say no more.

- Matt walked about in bathroom in mucky slippers so floor got muddy.
- I washed floor.
- This morning Matt took other bath toys (previously also a bit muddy) which I had washed and put them on the floor. Floor wet again.
- I dried floor.
- On leaving the house I reminded Matt, "Turn off light at your side of the bed, open the curtains and I've set up the clothes dryer for the wet washing which is in washing machine". Matt gave me 'the look'. I withered, realising I'm no longer meant to do things like this.
- He came out with me to the car (this is at 6.45am), opened the door and out fell Daisy's brand new white, frilly, expensive skirt into the gutter. Aaaaaargh! I slammed the door a bit and drove off, then stopped the car an hour later and sent a text to say sorry.

BUT ... WHAT! AM I NOT SUPPOSED TO SAY ANYTHING OR WHAT!

At night I played Scrabble with my dad for our usual tenner a game. We get together for a highly competitive game of Scrabble every month or so and play up to three games for a tenner a time. The third game can be double or quits depending on the outcome of the previous two games, so there is the possibility of winning or losing £40 in an evening. This is the only form of gambling I indulge in and I tend to think of it as fun 'work' as both of us make so much effort to win. It wasn't until dad had gone home (£10 richer – we were shattered after one extremely close game) that it occurred to me I should have perhaps asked Matt if it was OK for me to play. It seems that independent decision making is extremely difficult to change.

Monday 6th April

Shockingly, surprisingly, against all odds and with fingers crossed and breath abated I must write ... I have nothing much to report. The atmosphere at home has been, if anything, more relaxed than normal despite throwing a 3rd birthday party for Daisy at the weekend. I've been consciously trying not to give orders, have been failing some of the time, but I think Matt is really appreciating the effort I am making. I 'think' I've also been taking a bit more care of my appearance (backed up by the comments made by a pupil's mum I ran into in the garden centre this morning who said she's heard about this month's challenge and she thought I certainly looked much smarter than usual .... She said this in a nice and tactful way and I still like her!). Being 'nice' seems to be paying off – Matt is being very attentive towards me, is not expecting me to do anything more than usual, is voluntarily doing his usual routine of bathing Daisy etc and is bringing me a cup of tea in bed as usual every morning. Strange – I thought this month was going to be a nightmare. I also expected it to be much, much more work, but so far it seems the only thing I have to be is 'nice'. Wonder how long I can keep that up?

I've just thought of something else Matt and I were talking about earlier. All of the previous challenges seem to be amalgamating into our psyches and much more vociferously than when we were actively participating in them. Although I have only walked around 5, 000 steps for the last 4 days I made a real effort today to get back up to my 10, 000 steps. Last month seemed to be such a success that I want to continue to improve my fitness. We've both been resisting spending much money since January and whereas I would normally go to the supermarket as soon as the fridge or freezer started looking the slightest bit bare, I now eke out our groceries and make meals out of what is in the cupboards whenever possible. I am saving a fortune and am not noticing any 'lack'. Matt says he spends a lot less at lunchtimes and on snacks and aims to actively save and reduce needless and mindless frittering of money. Now if only we both looked polished at all times we'd really be hitting our targets!

Saturday 11th April

The exercise routine I started last month continues. I'm still doing my 10, 000 steps a day despite a four day break at the start of the month. I've also continued with press ups and sit ups and am now adding very strange looking but I think effective arm exercises taught to me by my dad. As an ex PTI (Physical Training instructor) in National Service and ex PE teacher I assumed he could give me some great training tips to improve my fitness. I almost laughed when he showed me his 'moves' as they seemed so antiquated and simple (I was expecting tips on using resistance bands or other fitness equipment) but my arms are already aching and I'm dead impressed with his advice. Again, as before, watch this space as I have no intention on weighing or measuring myself till the end of the month.

Back to submissive wife month. The strangest, strangest thing has happened - nothing's happened! I expected this to be a really explosive month, but we're getting on GREAT. We've been entertaining our friends; have been out and about for meals and days out and we've not bickered at all which is highly unusual for us. I received a phone call from my dad today to tell me he'd very badly broken his ankle while out fishing on his holidays. Naturally I was very worried. Matt expressed his concern too, but later added that it was especially sad that my dad was out of action for a while as he was hoping he'd babysit! He had been planning to take me away to a lovely country house hotel for a romantic break. I'm feeling a bit like Bridget Jones who found her Mr Darcy at the moment. Lovely.

P.S. I've got no idea if this marital-type harmony has actually got anything to do with our challenges. I may have to look at this in more depth retrospectively or, in other words, when or if I go back to my old nagging and compulsive list-making self.

Monday 13th April

Marital discord has occurred. This morning I was lying in bed with Matt discussing (somewhat smugly) how surprised I was at how well this challenge is going. He laughed, "Well you've hardly been a submissive wife". Ha ha ha. Instead of shouting back all the things I had on my mind like, 'have you no idea how much I've bitten my tongue the past two weeks, haven't you noticed how you've had more action than in the previous 6 months, are you aware that bugger all's been done in the house by you in the past fortnight, haven't you enjoyed all the extra special meals I've been making, are you aware of how many DVDs you've had the chance to watch and, most of all, were you not aware of how bloody NICE I've been?' All this I kept to myself whilst trying to stop the tears from escaping. I'm bloody mad. Clearly Matt doesn't think I've been submissive but I think I've been making big bloody strides towards it. Is this how most women used to feel – bloody insignificant and disregarded – I guess so. Rant over – got to go and empty the washing machine and do the dishes!

6.15pm

The day has gone from bad to worse. Humungous fight earlier in the car resulting in me telling Matt to get out then driving round the corner to cool off – even I'm not cruel enough to leave him stranded in the middle of the Borders without public transport to get him home. Anyway I won't go into details, but let's just say I'm totally hacked off. Not only do I feel like I've been doing everything in the house but the fact that it's not in any way returned (I'm ignoring the things he was going to plan … not nice I know, but the mood I'm in just now) is turning me into a frustrated madwoman. I'm dying to have a fight but know it wouldn't be nice and wifely. At the moment I've just brought in the washing (which I did earlier), put screen wash in the car, cleaned up dirty mirrors we brought down from the attic earlier, swept the whole house and am just cooking the basmati rice to go with the cooked-from-scratch vindaloo curry. Bitter, moi? F***, no!

Tuesday 14th April

It's almost half way through the month and due to recent circumstances I have decided to review this challenge with an aim to making any changes necessary to maintain some sort of harmony over the next two weeks. Matt and I have done so much talking over the last day or two… let me rephrase that … Matt and I have done so much talking in between huge sullen silences over the last couple of days that we have come to the following conclusions:

- Neither of us knows what we are doing this month
- We cannot come to any kind of consensus about the definition of a submissive or surrendered wife
- We both think I find it incredible difficult to relinquish control. Again, we both think I need to learn to do this (to what extent we still have to negotiate!)
- We both think it would be good for Matt to make more decisions on what we do with our time/domestic arrangements/social life etc but again, we have varying ideas of how urgently or quickly these things would be arranged (I've been trying so hard not to keep nagging him about looking at my laptop which has been broken for the last 7 months even though he has been fixing other people's computers during this time out of the goodness of his heart – shades of cobblers children's shoes?)
- Matt rightly expressed his concern that if I want him to organise our social life I have to stop jumping in and doing it myself first. I replied, "of course" before hastily telling him we are going to Morag and Ben's for dinner tomorrow night and that a work colleague and her husband are coming to ours in a couple of weeks. Apart from that, I'll stop.
- We have questioned why we are doing this challenge. Or rather, Matt has questioned why we are doing this challenge. I said I think we could both use some of the appropriate yin/yang qualities we are perhaps a tad short in. Matt doesn't seem so sure. 'If it ain't broke...'

and all that... and if it is broke he doesn't really want to have to think about it.

- I thought we might have some fun with this challenge. We're not. Well not over the last couple of days anyway.

Deep breath. For the next couple of weeks I'm going to try to keep my big maw shut. I'm going to leave all social and domestic arrangements to Matt and am going to try really, really hard not to give him any instructions (apparently I'm still unconsciously doing this ALL THE TIME). Can't recall him saying he was going to try anything!

Monday 20th April

Well, all quiet on the Western front at this end. Amazingly we have been getting on pretty well over the past few days. This really is a rollercoaster ride challenge month. I'm reading a book at the moment about one of the wives in a polygamist marriage and don't know if I feel glad not to be part of what, at times can seem like a barbaric sect or wishing I had the support, friendship and joint effort provided by having several 'sisters'. Not quite sure how Matt would manage to woo the other 18 wives as well though, considering how difficult he seems to be finding it to arrange for a babysitter to take me out for one evening.

Tuesday 21st April

Matt asked tonight why I was chewing gum. Taken aback by the question I kind of stuttered for an answer. "Is it for the taste?" he continued to ask. "I guess so," I replied. He suggested I try mints instead. I assumed he was telling me I looked like I was chewing the cud, so I did what any reasonable woman would do – I went through the kitchen and cried. Now, on a normal day I would have told him to mind his own bloody business but being the non-confrontational person I've been attempting to be I said nothing but am instead deeply, deeply hurt. I HATE this challenge.

Thursday 23rd April
Once again previous challenges are coming together. I am continuing with my 10, 000 steps a day and am starting to feel much fitter. Matt has convinced me to have one day's rest a week so (doing as I'm told) as long as I cover 60, 000 steps over a week I'm happy. I've also upped my sit ups to 30 a day and continue with the 20 push ups and arm exercises. The concept of the challenges seems to be spreading. The pupils in my school are incredibly interested in my progress and it seems this interest has been passed to some of the parents. I am often asked by parents at the end of the school day how the month's challenge is going, but today I had a parent come into the school to tell me their family had been discussing the challenges and have set their own for this month. They are going to put everything back in the house from where they found it. She told me how hard the family were finding it but were really enjoying challenging themselves. I'm so chuffed …. I've always wanted to be a guru for a day! In case you're wondering how I broached the subject of this month's challenge – I didn't really! – I told my pupils I was trying to do the best job I possibly could at looking after my house and family – as a very, very proud and political feminist I'm hardly likely to ever use the words 'submissive' and 'wife' as a positive role model for anyone.

Friday 24th April

Tonight I hinted to Matt that our friends Seonaid and George said they'd keep Daisy for an overnight stay ANYTIME. I also let him know that other friends, Myra and John had a free weekend. All this information I left in his hands.

Saturday 25th April

It worked. Matt booked us an overnight stay tonight in the smartest country house hotel in the area. He got us a deal for the honeymoon suite, packed Daisy off to Seonaid and George, packed a bottle of champagne and booked dinner for eight o'clock. Wow. He didn't even blink when I said I wasn't keen on the honeymoon suite they gave us (very big, separate living room, bedroom, dressing room and bathroom but green and yellow are not the colours for me – too cold) and happily downgraded to a room I preferred (nicer colours and they brought us all the accoutrements such as tea and coffee making facilities, ice bucket, etc). Yes, yes, I know I'm not meant to complain, but when done in a nice way I think I can almost get away with it (an excuse I know). I packed my Hotel Chocolat chocolates and amazed Matt by sharing them with him.

The real luxury of the weekend was having time to spend with each other. We talked, laughed, walked hand in hand, made plans for the future and felt closer to each other than we have for ages. Money well spent. When we left the hotel we set off for the garden centre (Daisy was off fishing with Seonaid, George and Rory) in preparation for our next challenge. We fortuitously bumped into Myra and John so invited them for dinner next weekend. We compared notes over the luxurious surroundings we'd just experienced (it was they who first convinced us to ask for the honeymoon suite) and discussed future plans for holidays, meals out and treats. It's so lovely to be pals with people who like to enjoy life to the hilt – I'm sure pleasure, like laughter is contagious.

Upon our return home I got back into challenge mode and went walking. Seonaid called me at night saying she too wants to start the walking challenge and has asked me to get her a super duper pedometer like mine. Even though I'd done my steps for the day we both went on a 4, 000 step walk round the back of the village. It's so much harder to walk and keep up a conversation – made me realise how much more women talk when they're together than we do with our men. Not exactly sure if Matt would want me to rectify that though!

Monday 27th April

Hardly feels like submissive wife month. I went out with the girls tonight for cocktails, dinner then onto a jazz club, but being the dedicated woman I am I 'attempted' my exercises (giggling all the while, Matt reports) upon my return at 1am.

Wednesday 29th April

I decided to follow up on last month's challenge and as this is almost the end of the month I did another weigh in and measure. I stood on the scales somewhat gingerly, expecting to have regained most of the weight lost last month due to the amount of meals out and chocolates I've been eating recently, but alas I had lost another 2lbs bringing my total lost to 12 lbs. I had also lost an inch from my bust, waist and hips and another half inch from each thigh. Feel like I've discovered the Holy Grail.

At night an even greater feat occurred. The boy sure did good! Just before the challenge draws to an end Matt arranged a babysitter and took me out for one of the loveliest meals I've ever had. We went to a very lovely Spanish restaurant, consumed two very fine bottles of wine and a truly scrumptious meal AND Matt insisted on paying for everything. What a way to end a challenge. We merrily returned home feeling very loved up and paid the babysitter, Matt retired to our bedroom and I did my sit ups, push ups, arm exercises and the 1, 500 steps I still had to do for the day. Dedicated or mad? I'll make it up to him later.

Postscript

A month of many ups and downs! I'm not sure this challenge was a success but I certainly enjoyed some of it (i.e. the last week). I've probably not relinquished much control though I have been making real efforts not to tell Matt how to do things. Matt, to my great surprise has started taking some decisions into his own hands and has looked at or fixed more things in the house than he would have from being nagged. Without constant badgering he's converted our videos to DVDs, looked at and ordered the part to fix my laptop, hung pictures and mirrors in the dining room and started ordering garden equipment and building materials for our next challenge. Have we retained our roles in any way at all? You will find out.

Chapter 5 – May

Create an Outdoor Space

This is a challenge we have both been looking forward to for some time and was planned to take place during what we hoped was the most suitable month for reaping rewards – not that we really know this. Neither Matt nor I can be called gardeners. I bought my lovely wee cottage in the country 22 years ago. It came with a gorgeous vegetable garden, little orchard and lots of lovely mature plants and trees. Within a few months I had managed to kill all but the hardiest of trees. Over the years I have planted numerous window boxes and planters and have experienced hours of pleasure from each and when I say hours I mean hours, not weeks. Neglect, ignorance, laziness – failure to thrive could be placed on any of the above, but surprisingly, even without me ever watering them, weeds continue to thrive in my garden.

Matt, new to country life and having never tended a garden before has, over the years, bought both 'How to be a Gardener' books by Alan Titmarsh. I can't actually vouch that he's opened them but they have come in really handy as big tablemats to protect our dining table.

What in the garden are we concentrating on? We don't know. We haven't got a clue how much is achievable in a month so we have taken 'before' shots and plan to take 'afters' presuming there is a noticeable difference to show you.

Now, things have changed for us quite dramatically since my last diary entry. On 1st May, Matt was officially put into the consultation period prior to being made redundant. We think this means he will actually be finished work anywhere from the next week to the next 5 or 6 weeks so …. We're not going to go ahead with any major spending on the garden for the moment. We did have great plan to buy water butts, guttering, etc and were hoping to renew all the wood on our big shed/workshop but this may not happen. This challenge may seem vague. We are too. About everything EXCEPT for the fact that we love each other, have the greatest daughter in the world, are in a much better position financially than loads of other people and were able to live on almost nothing during January's challenge and could do again if necessary. So, s**t happens – we are counting our blessings.

Sunday 3rd May

Glorious, glorious weather! After a second full day in the garden the grass has had its first cut of the year, one whole side of the garden in front of the conifers has been weeded (at this point I must interject that while I write conifers I actually have no idea if this is the correct name – please follow this excuse as with all other mentions of plants I make during this month), six bucket bags full of weeds have been picked, some broken planters have been thrown away and Matt has started demolishing our crappy, old, coal bunker (a total health and safety hazard with rusting cut metal and old bits of wood attached to the front) in readiness for putting up our new one (ordered before last week's shock announcement). I've not managed to walk my 10, 000 steps a day but am absolutely knackered already so think I may end up swapping gardening for walking this month. Having said that, I'm extremely obstinate so as I'm still within the 60, 000 for the week I've not actually failed yet. Wait, wait, I'm starting to become obsessive – I passed that challenge and am only continuing with it because I loved the results. But, may I say, particularly in times of stress such as these, it's been fantastic to have my challenges to take my mind off our problems.

Monday 11th May

It's been a long time between diary entries but this is proving to be an exhausting and extremely difficult challenge. The Great British weather ensures that we can often only garden sporadically and so in order to complete 10 hours a week each in the garden we have had to virtually live outside on clear days. Today I feel like I've been doing a hundred sit ups and in fact I've missed my exercises for at least 4 of the past 7 days. I have continued to do my steps but this particular kind of fitness means relatively little when you have to spend the day digging. Over the past few days I have weeded most of the cottage garden and have planted containers, window boxes and borders with a selection of annual and perennial plants. For the first time I actually spent some time planning what should go to the back or the front of the borders according to size, but I wish I knew more about which plants will come back every year. I'm assuming that they don't unless they have perennial on the label, but who knows. I chose what to buy according to what I quite liked the look of and I think I have a selection of daisies, pansies, lupins, sweet peas, delphiniums, hollyhocks and lots of other things I've already forgotten the names of. I was a bit extravagant in the garden centre spending just over a hundred quid, but that included a willow partition to hopefully keep our neighbour's cat out of our garden. I said as much to my neighbour, whose cat uses our garden as a toilet. She insisted her cat must be too old to jump over the existing fence but was faced with the embarrassment later of seeing that her cat had climbed up our newly painted wall and had the offending paw prints from our house to hers. Ha!

Matt used the weekend to get out all his pent up frustration. He demolished our old coal bunker, painted part of the outside of the house, hammered up the partition and shovelled bagfuls of old earth and rubbish. I think physically exhausting yourself helps reduce strain and certainly makes you too exhausted to have your mind wandering at night. I keep thinking about two different books I read many years ago where snippets of gardening metaphors keep popping into my head. The first was by Alice Walker and was, I think, from 'In Search of my Mother's Garden'. It may have been a short story or a novel, I can't remember, but the message was that no matter what we have or what is happening in our lives we can help things to nourish and grow with care, nurturing and love. Alice Walker recalled her mother's real and wondrous garden as well as the emotional support, care and love she received from her mother. The other excerpt which often flashes in my mind is of Voltaire in 'Candide' saying, and I do not quote, first we must tend our own garden and although I know he meant this metaphorically I think our family will benefit from the fresh air, hard physical work and convergence with nature that this more literal translation will afford us.

Sunday 17th May

The challenge has taken a turn for the worse, for me anyway. Although I had done some mid-week gardening I was off work on Friday and may possibly be off tomorrow as I initially had a sore throat and now have a really, really sore back. I think it's a virus. I've hardly been able to move since Thursday night so gardening is most certainly out for me. The weekend has been a complete write-off. Not only have I been unable to do anything in the garden but I have absolutely no patience for looking after Daisy so Matt isn't getting a chance to do much either. We took a drive to Berwick yesterday and bought the materials for doing the roof so at least when Matt gets a chance to get something done he won't have to stop to go and get materials.

P.S. My walking and exercise has also taken a complete back seat. I've done nothing for the last three days but so I don't seize up completely I'm going to try to go out for a walk tonight.

Monday 25th May

The entries in this part of my diary are becoming few and far between. The one thing we have discovered beyond any shadow of a doubt is that you CANNOT put a time allowance on how long you will spend in the garden during the Great British spring or summer. Rain has stopped play for many of the days so far and although we are trying to make up on the clear days we are certainly not managing to stick rigidly to our schedule. Matt (for once) is sticking to his challenge much better than I am. He has spent lots of time out of doors trimming hedges, erecting a new coal bunker, painting and cutting up and dumping rubbish. Unfortunately when he is doing that I have to look after Daisy and so the things I am doing are limited. True, she has helped me plant seeds and flowers and sort of 'helps' water the garden but anything which requires a bit more exertion or would require me being in the front garden are out of bounds as I cannot trust her not to wander onto the road.

Our personal life is still on a roller-coaster ride. Over the last couple of weeks Matt's notice of redundancy has been put on hold and we've gone from him maybe going to Ireland, then Wales and now probably to London to work for a while. Whether this will save his job or not is anyone's guess. In the meantime I'm fretting about time away from him and if I hadn't promised the kids in my class that I was going to try not to watch telly next month (which they are all very excited about tracking) then I would certainly be switching the challenges around. I'm absolutely fed up to think I may be stuck in the house for a month on my own with NO TELLY and no Matty for company. Would happily settle for either and of course would much rather have my lovely man, but … I'll miss the final of the Apprentice, Britain's Next Top Model and, I never thought I'd admit this but I've just watched an episode of Britain's Got Talent or 'Britain Exploits the Mentally Challenged' (as Matthew Wright calls it) and I could easily get hooked on this trash TV.

Sunday 31st May

The day from hell! But I'll come back to that later. On Friday I hosted our book group at the cottage so I could show off our lovely garden. This was booked two months in advance and shows the optimism I had when making arrangements. Well, I did host the book club. It was lovely and we did sit outside. However it wasn't in a completely transformed garden with new patio, freshly painted and roofed sheds with a lovely weed-free rolling lawn and cleared area at the back of the garden. Rather, it was in a 'nice' garden with loads of newly planted plants, tubs and with a semi-finished divider between our garden and next door. Oh, and a new coal bunker and about a third of a trimmed garden full of hedges and plants. The front garden looked OK too, with newly cut hedges and new tubs, but, boy oh boy, were we disappointed at how little of a difference our labours made! It's true we didn't stick exactly to the hours expected – weather dictated we couldn't always do that, but because we'd not touched the garden at all yet this year we spent the entire month basically fire fighting. One of our book group ladies laughed when I explained our plans we had for the month and wasn't at all surprised that we barely touched the surface.

Overall we feel we've made a start and are planning to make this a lifetime's labour (maybe, of love, I've not quite decided yet, but Matt is certainly more keen than me). Did we pass the challenge? Matt certainly did but I probably didn't if time spent was the criteria for passing. In the summary section are some of our before and after shots – you decide. As for the day from hell comments – I'll explain shortly.

Did we succeed? You decide...

Before ... (should I be ashamed?)

After

Chapter 6 – June

Indecisions, Indecisions!

Was meant to be 'no telly month'

Read on....

I feel really guilty. This month we were meant to go without watching any telly. Not everyone has faith in my abilities to do that one. See the musings below from Joanna, one of my primary 2 pupils in regard to, not only a similar challenge she set herself, but her thoughts on how she expects me to manage in the month ahead (I do realise this may be a bit tricky to decipher, both due to the size of the writing or because you've not read a lot of writing from 5 or 6 year olds, so I have written the exact transcript underneath – go on, give it a go!)

"I am not going to watch tv for the whole weekend".

E did Pas my chalinsh and it was to not woch eny tv. I found it roolly hard when it miss mcgregor chalinsh for a month to woch no tv I thinck sheel find it roolly hard beacaus I found it farto hard but I manisht it. It was roolly tempting not watching Horrid hennry and it is my fafrit program. Thats why it was really tempting so miss mcgregor wont manich it. And she wont beabolto woch hr fafrit programs I thinck she wont beabol to dowit. I bet shel woch it ect leest once. Thats wot I think. And it is for all of June I just wonder Low she will manich to dow it. Like dowing daddy he can woch no tv or miss wois tee. beacaus miss mcgregor tori and hu clos i dont no how daisy dowisly dosit when miss mcgor said to I coulnt beacwis I didnt no is she was mine fre room. How is she going to dow it now. Why did she wont to do a colihun to woch no tv how on erth is she going to dowi it how on erth will she dowit how on erth is she is she going to pass it now she wont pass I now she wont Pass I how it I dow I dow I dow I dow How will she dow it I bet is I dow no a exit Eeeee

"I did pas my chalinsh and it was to not woch eny tv. I found it roolly hard when it miss mcgregors chalinsh for a month. To woch no tv I thinck sheel find it roolly hard beacaus I found it farto hard but I manisht it. It was roolly tempting. Not watching Horrid hennry. And it is my fafrit program. Thats why it was really tempting so miss mcgregor wont manich it. And she wont beabolto woch hr fafrit programs I thinck she wont beabol to dowit. I bet shel woch it ect leest once. Thats wot I think. And it is for all of June I just wonder

76

how she will manij it. Shel not dow it. Like daisys daddy he can woch no tv for his hole life. Beacaus miss mcgor told the hole class. I don't no how daisys daddy dosit wen miss mcgor told us I coodint bleevit I didint no if she was tlling the troot. How is she going to do it now. Why did she want to do a calinch to woch no tv how an erth is she going to dowi it how an erth will she dow it how an erth is she is she going to pass I now she wont pass I now she wont pass I now it I dow I dow I dow I dow. How will she dow it I don't no I don't no a tall not a tall".

And all I can say to this is I'm both delighted and flabbergasted to have piqued a very young pupil's interest so much to have generated such a considered response (even if she does sound rather like a character from Father Ted!) ... and, in Joanna's defence, her usually impeccable spelling was uncharacteristically forgotten as her response so very freely flowed.

Well .... Joanna's doubts aside ... and I've got to say they started creeping into my own psyche ... This month's challenge has been changed for several reasons and if I start writing my innermost thoughts at the moment I'll never stop crying so here they are in a very formal 'list':

- Matt is being moved to London with his job rather than face immediate redundancy. This stinks and we'll only see each other at weekends. We're not sure how long this is for but at least a month.

- Yesterday, whilst away for the weekend, we found Daisy playing with a half-opened packet of unidentifiable tablets she had found. Panic ensued resulting in a very traumatic trip to the Sick Kids Hospital in Edinburgh. She hadn't eaten any (we later found out), but the trip into Edinburgh when she kept falling asleep (through heat and lack of sleep from the excitement of her holiday) made the journey the most frightening experience of my life.

- The Apprentice final is in 10 days and I really don't want to miss it.
- I'm so fed up at the moment I don't want to deprive myself of anything else.

Sounds fairly pathetic I know but our current situation has dictated that we have a re-think of the challenges and their timing, so this month we're going to spend the whole month looking at our finances. There – just when you thought it couldn't get any more exciting!

So,

June

Money, Money, Money (which fits in very well with Daisy's current obsession with our friend's Mamma Mia DVD – perhaps at the end of the month I'll feel flush enough to buy her one of her own)!

Monday 8th June

It's been quite a productive last few days. I've been spending loads of time on Martin Lewis's internet finance site (http://www.moneysavingexpert.com) and have been looking at the ins and outs of investments and savings. Although I have managed to grasp the advice about what you should do if the market is in a state of inflation or deflation, the moment I think I'm sorted the whole concept seems to miraculously escape me again and I feel as ignorant as ever. However I have checked out the best interest rates we can expect for our savings and ISAs and have today closed old accounts which were doing particularly badly and will open new accounts when the money is transferred later in the week.

We want this challenge to be more than thinking about how to best invest any savings we have and to even stretch ourselves past looking for ways to save on our expenses but also to be about how we can generate more income in the future. I'm planning to spend the next week enquiring about tutoring for the Open University. Both Matt and I are interested in further education and having done my original degree with the Open University, I am passionate about its ethos. I've heard the money is pretty poor but if we both enjoyed it and felt we were benefiting professionally then any amount would be a bonus.

Sunday 14th June

Well I watched the final of the Apprentice last week and it was so not worth it. I sometimes stun myself with my ability to spend so much time in front of the telly. However the last couple of months have been a tremendous strain and I've been feeling completely shattered lately so justify my time spent on our (new and very comfy) sofa accordingly.

And ….. We've just found out another reason for the tiredness – I'm pregnant. We're kind of shell-shocked and it hasn't really sunk in, but … what timing … Matt on verge of redundancy and me, well …. Very, very old! Having said that, we're both thrilled and very nervous as I miscarried twins late last year. Fingers crossed.

Everything else pales in comparison with that news but we both looked up how to apply as Open University tutors and worked out the pay scales we could expect.

One of us is clearly not too bright because as we compared notes this morning we had both read differently into the information provided on the website.

I have also had a few moments of organisation this week. My old ISA account has been transferred into the highest earning new ISA I could find (well almost the highest. I still wanted to bank with a company I had heard of and who was not based abroad in case anything went wrong – I know in theory your money could be covered but how difficult to try to deal with things in another country in potentially a different language).

It's good that we are looking after our finances, but it kind of blows all our efforts out of the water with the fact that we might be having a very, very expensive little bundle coming along soon!

Dear Reader, do not expect much more input this month. I know I've hardly written so far, but it's the end of term, things are becoming frantic at school and, well, I need all the extra sleep I can muster at the moment.

Wednesday 17th June

Scary, scary! I've just filled in an application to open an online bank account for the first time. Feel so brave (I know it's pathetic but I'm joining the 21st century very, very slowly). Mind you, I made Matt sit beside me when I was typing out my answers in case I needed any help. In case any parents of the children I teach are reading this, they should probably stop now or they may be nervous for the intellectual welfare or at least the technological abilities of their children for the future! Off now to have a nice cup of tea to relax. Decaf.

Friday 19th June

F*!* – just as you think it can't get any worse. I came home from work yesterday to several answering machine messages from the doctors' surgery asking me to call back. It turns out that two abnormalities have shown up on a gynaecological scan I had last week. I brushed that aside and told the doctor I had found out 2 days after my scan that I was pregnant so I was expecting a call from him. That's not what showed up though, he explained. I questioned him further and he said there's a black spot which looks as if it could be endometriosis which doesn't worry him at all because that is usually only ever treated if it's causing problems. Unfortunately one of my ovaries is a different size to the others though and looks spongy. The doctor said they may next expect to do an MRI scan but he's not sure they'll do that now that I'm pregnant. He told me not to worry – he's writing to the hospital for a quick follow up BUT I'm scared shitless. I feel like I may be facing a horrible decision ahead (thinking as almost all would of worst case scenario – but how could anyone help but doing that?). F***, f***, f*!*! Trying not to stress too much as that can't be good for pregnancy. How much more in the way of tests can we face just now?

Wednesday 24th June

Brilliant news - the consultant from the hospital phoned me yesterday and told me there is nothing to worry about with my scan results. True, there are cystic spaces, I am informed, but they should not cause me any worry and nothing else needs to be done unless I experience any pain. She says she'll look again at my 12 week pregnancy scan.

This book has taken a real back seat over the last couple of weeks – as has everything else. I've stopped recording my steps and am not at all sure I'm doing close to 10 000 a day, but I'm so bloody tired at the moment I can hardly do anything else. My sit ups, press ups and arm curls stopped weeks ago and as for trying them again, ditto. I'm hoping to catch up on rest over the holidays (only one day of school left) then I'll hopefully reinstate all my previous good efforts. As for this month's challenge – we can safely say we've failed. We were meant to be finding out about extra ways to make money and were going to look into grants for building/environmental things such as solar panels, making extra income, potential future grants for Matt for help with software etc for partially sighted people, but … for the moment we just want to sit back, take a deep breath and be grateful we're healthy, love each other and have a great and hopefully expanding family.

Tuesday 30th June
'The month of highs and lows', as this chapter should be called, continues. Matt was finally made redundant today. He has a month's notice to work and although we're going camping later in the week, our guess is that they won't expect him in the office for the whole month when he comes back. I certainly tried to put a brave face on it and talked about how we'd spend time together in the holidays and how this could be the chance to try being self employed etc, but by the end of the night the strain had started to show and we had a few words, I had a few tears (as in truth I'm scared shitless about being pregnant with potentially no money coming in from Matt for a long time). However we quickly apologised and went to bed talking (well, Matt went to bed and I've stayed up to watch telly till as

close to midnight as I can since next month is going to be no telly month. As for this month's challenge – considering our finances – I don't need to think about our finances any bloody more for the moment, thank you very much. We can safely say this month has been a disaster – in almost every sense of the word – bar the new baby of course – the light at the end of our very long tunnel (along with our wee darling Daisy of course).

Chapter 7 – July

No Telly

As you know this challenge was meant to happen last month. The very fact that I changed it should be some indication of how hard I expect to find this task. I watch telly a lot. It goes on in the morning for The Wright Stuff most days and then is invariably on again in the evening for almost anything from 8 o'clock onwards. If we're at the flat in Edinburgh then there is also the added temptation of Sky so anything from Britain's Next Top Model to Oprah can be on most days. At the cottage we have a very bare choice of Sky freebie channels (which is now free after paying for the initial installation) so we do tend to watch a lot less telly there.

I decided to make this month no telly AND no videos and DVDs otherwise I knew I'd end up renting a couple of DVDs a day – which just wouldn't be right – and you know how hard I've tried to stick to my challenges – well, some of them. I have decided to allow trips to the cinema as this is a social occasion and is quite different to being slumped in front of a goggle box. Overall this month I'd like to see if the quality of my life improves without telly. How much more will I get done? Will it be worth it?

Monday 6th July

Well almost a week has passed and it's gone in unbelievably quickly. Although I have had a couple of pangs of wanting to put the telly on I have resisted. It's been much easier with us having gone camping for two days. I've also read a book and a couple of magazines and last night, for almost the first time ever, I went to bed when I was tired rather than when the telly programmes finished. The fact that it was half past eight does admittedly seem rather sad, but … I'm pregnant so have a perfect excuse. Tonight we have Morag, Ben and Solomon coming round for dinner – I hope tennis-mad Ben doesn't want to watch Wimbledon or I'll have to leave the room (as I had to do when dad watched the news at the cottage yesterday). And, in case you think I'm depriving Daisy during this challenge (though I'd argue it was a deprivation), she is still able to watch a little telly every day. Far from being an anti-telly mum, I think some of the children's programmes are wonderful.

Tuesday 7th July

Had a lovely night last night with Morag, Ben and Sol. I absolutely love our wee Edinburgh dining room – it's perfect for a very, very intimate dinner party. We discovered today that we should make the most of it just now because very soon we won't be able to use it at all. We're expecting twins! I'm seven and a half weeks pregnant. At least this may go some way to explaining why I am absolutely shattered. Although up to a few weeks ago I had been doing my 10 000 steps a day, for the last three weeks or so I have found it a real effort to get up to speed again and have failed most days. No bloody wonder. I already see a change in my body – not fat exactly but sturdiness just under my bust. Oh crikey – as if I need to put on any more weight. We're both extremely shell-shocked and more than a little nervous not least due to the fact that I miscarried twins last October. So – we'll try not to get too excited or to worry too much if we can because it's early doors and there's still a long way to go till I can relax a bit. As for

85

telly watching – or lack of telly watching – it hasn't even entered my head at the moment. So far a successful challenge – and about time too – the challenges or success rate of the challenges was beginning to get me down. After all I am hoping to try these new measures to make a lasting impact on my life for the better. Just a thought – it now looks like I'll be able to use my economy drive skills and walking habits much more in the future as we may be far too poor to afford a car!

Wednesday 8th July

I seem to be finding lots of time to write just now which is hardly surprising. I put Daisy into nursery this afternoon (she now only goes one afternoon a week when I am not working) and promptly came back to bed for a wee snooze. For once I don't even feel guilty about it. At the moment I'm lying in bed with the laptop savouring the last hour's peace before she returns with Matt, both probably tired, cranky and looking for dinner. I've been looking up the internet about twins and there are lots of things which hadn't really crossed my mind before. For example, testing – apparently high hormone levels render blood tests inaccurate and as for amniocentesis – what do you do if only one has a problem? Cripes – lots to consider. I have an appointment with my consultant in two weeks in the Borders General Hospital so I'm going to start getting questions ready.

It feels strange lying relaxing without watching telly but I must say I'm quite enjoying it. I feel like I've got all the time in the world to look at all the different things I'm thinking about just now and am logging onto the internet at least a couple of times a day (and I promise I'm not watching iPlayer or catch-up t.v. for the other channels). I've been quickly replying to correspondence from my friend and fellow book club member Joan who is at the moment in Australia and have spent lots of time contacting pals including my old dentist and drinking buddy Claire who now lives in the Isle of Mann and who is coming to stay with me tonight. I think telly has helped disconnect me from people and it is nice reconnecting.

Monday 13th July

We've just had a great weekend camping with Ben, Morag and Sol on the Northumbrian coast. We stayed at Budle Bay and went trips to Bamburgh and Alnwick. The lack of telly has not really affected my life. Whether this is because we are doing so many other things, or whether we are doing so many other things because I am not watching telly, I am not sure. I do know I spent my evening differently tonight than I would normally do. When Matt returned from work we had a lovely dinner then I took off for the cinema and happily watched 'The Secret Lives of Pippa Lee' whilst drinking a coffee and munching on a packet of Fruit Gums. What I do know is that it felt completely unlike sitting in front of the telly. It was 'an occasion', a 'treat' and I thoroughly enjoyed the couple of hours to myself, the complete escapism and the leisurely dander back via Waitrose to pick up a few messages. I am now at home ensconced in front of the computer and it is only 9.15pm. I'm even looking forward to going to bed to start my new novel (having finished another one this afternoon). Can't pretend I am particularly broadening my mind with literature in no-telly month as so far I have been exclusively reading murder stories. My next two books are however, an African classic 'Things Fall Apart' and a light-hearted book about raising twins (to hopefully help dispel my fears). So, to bed … or I may dabble a bit with some paint as I spent an art and craft day with Daisy today while the weather was yucky and I thought I might have a wee go myself with the canvasses I bought a couple of years ago and which have been gathering dust ever since.

Tuesday 14th July
Can't believe it is only one day from my last diary entry and that things are so different. I am BORED, BORED, BORED and REALLY, REALLY WANT TO WATCH TELLY. I've been out walking all day and have completed my 10 000 steps for the first time in ages and now I am well and truly exhausted and more than anything else want to completely collapse in front of the box. Morag gave me some good old trashy magazines today and I'm already on my third. I've also read three quarters of my book on twins but neither of these is hitting the spot. I don't even care what I'd be watching – in a dreamlike state I'm imagining The Wright Stuff, Loose Woman, Masterchef or Britain's Next Top Model – real no-thinking-required-just-sit-back-and-enjoy telly. Ah well, 17 days to go – Matt says I will have broken the habit by then. He should try to do the same with his computer and a little game called Travian (which he vehemently denies takes up any real time and claims helps with strategic thinking – my bottom it does)!

Friday 17th July
I made my second trip to a cinema in a week last night – not for any urgency to see a film, may I add, but for a desperate need to escape my moaning little daughter who was severely trying my patience over dinner. After cooking a beautiful roast dinner with all the

trimmings and with lovely juicy honey mangoes for dessert the last thing I wanted to hear was, "I don't like dinner" said at least 50 times before a mouthful was taken. So I escaped to see 'Bruno', the new movie from Sasha Baron Cohen and it was absolutely rubbish. I would have walked out except I remembered in time what I would be walking back to!

Matt has a meeting with an agency in Glasgow today with a view to finding him a job on an Edinburgh surveying project. He's also guaranteed an interview with the council on a job if he meets all the relevant criteria. He's not sure if he does – it's for an asset manager – but we were both quite surprised that people are able to positively discriminate for a post. He had to tick a box to say if he wanted to get a definite interview and although Matt would normally be too proud to even mention his disability at first, in this current climate of the worst recession Britain has seen for many years, he knows it would be foolish to ignore possibly the only way to equalise the initial disadvantage he has been shown by the majority of companies in his previous search for jobs. Although most companies are smart enough not to say it matters he had a few who openly said they wouldn't be able to work with his disability (even though this has in actuality caused him little or no problems in the past).

Back to the effects of the challenge for the month – the house is the cleanest it has been for a long time, I've cleaned out cupboards which we used to store stuff in when we moved in two and a half years ago, we've been eating beautifully prepared meals every night (nothing quick and easy, rather full roast dinners, roast gammon to turn into pasta dishes, etc) and Daisy's room is being gutted on a regular basis. Is it worth it? I'll tell you at the end of the month.

7.30pm same evening

Bored, bored, bored again. Just had a complete hissy fit at Matt, brought on no doubt by Daisy's grumping again at dinner. Plus he seems to be putting in more time and effort than ever at work and I don't see the point as he's getting no bloody thanks for it at all. I may have a bad attitude but if my work were treating me the same way then I'd definitely have different priorities. In bed typing this as was going to go a drive to Borders Books but don't feel I can justify buying new books just now unless heavily discounted on Amazon. Will go round second hand shops tomorrow to see what I can pick up.

Monday 20th July

At last I've started to put my non-telly watching to good use. For the third time in a row (all within the last fortnight), I've won a tenner from dad at Scrabble. My brain must be rejuvenating itself from lack of zombified telly watching. We are also achieving some quite spectacular achievements on the DIY front at home too. Today Matt and dad painted the outside of the cottage and the whole place is beginning to look rather lovely – fitting in quite well with my nesting instinct which is kicking in just now. Now also well and truly into my fifth book of the month (and I've read every magazine given to me by friends from cover to cover – I'm even tempted to look at Matt's Custom PC magazine – just joking, not that desperate yet!

Thursday 23rd July

Only 8 days to go till I can watch telly again and I probably don't even have to give you a heads up about what my decision will be. I'm absolutely sure I will watch telly again, though I hope I will be more selective in my viewing. I am certainly managing to achieve a lot more on the domestic front. My house is looking pretty tidy and I've at last gotten around to doing some of the wee jobs I've been putting off for ages such as hanging pictures, getting photos printed for photo frames, making curtains for the bathroom glass door (to the relief of at least one diner at every meal in our wee dining room who can see into the bathroom at inopportune times) and sorting out cupboards around the house. However, has my quality of life improved? No, I don't think so. The advantages gained by having a tidier house and garden are probably offset against my lack of feeling completely 'relaxed'. I feel 'on' all the time and am constantly looking for something to do, a new challenge or searching the internet for something interesting to read. The very fact that I have been doing school work during my summer holidays attests to the fact that I do not feel sufficiently 'switched off'.

So what am I going to do for the remaining 8 days? Well I might as well make the most of the 'research' time I have available to me. I will continue to do school work for the next few days, after which I can completely switch off and not look at it again till I'm back in school. I'll also continue to clean the house and may even attempt another painting (and may even attempt something more difficult than an abstract pattern) to hang in my beautifully tidy living room. After that, shall I make a frilly apron to go alongside my vaguely 'Stepford-like' resemblance or shall I switch on the telly? You guess!

Tuesday 28th July
'Nothing much to report', I write semi-guiltily. I have not turned on or over a telly channel since this

challenge began. I have also positioned myself away from TV screens when in bars with a telly on the wall. I've even asked friends to turn their tellies off if they weren't watching them, or explained I would have to leave the room. Why, oh why then did I not notice that our friend Sue who was babysitting for us had the telly on when we returned from our night out (sober I may add – remember my condition). Anyway, she was watching a programme about Michael Jackson which I had seen before, yet … completely unconsciously I watched … or should I say stared at the screen for several minutes. In reality this may have only been a minute or two and it was certainly passive staring rather than active viewing BUT I am still bloody annoyed with myself AND I had not even realised it till I went to bed at night. So I'm calling it a blip and having beaten myself up loads overnight (as if I have not bigger things to worry about at the moment) and am still going to claim I am succeeding at my challenge. I'm also getting quite excited about Saturday night. Not because I'm putting on my glad rags and going out dancing but because I'm going to buy a big bar of chocolate or make Mars Bar slices and sit in front of the telly for several hours AND I don't even know what's on yet!

On a note in which I should be more worried than about telly, Matt is now officially unemployed having had his last day at work today. We would toast our new life with a glass of bubbly but if you think about the amount of time I worry about trivial things just think how I'd be about drinking or eating naughty foods in pregnancy.

Wednesday 29th July
Matt's first day as a newly redundant man and his bloody work have already been phoning to ask him

questions. I was so pleased – he didn't respond to their message and will make them wait till tomorrow. This is all because they paid so little attention when he was trying to pass work over to them and now they want him to help them out when he is no longer paid and has only been given the minimum statutory redundancy. I should bloody hope not.

Anyway we spent the afternoon holding hands at the cinema. We probably should have gone to see a soppy romantic movie or a laugh-a-minute comedy but instead I dragged Matt to see a depressing but excellent film about a struggling single mother who helps smuggle illegal aliens across the Canadian border in order to make ends meet. 'Entertainment?' you may ask – it takes all types!

The month is clearly drawing to a close. I think I've been to the cinema at least 5 times and am on at least my 6th or 7th book yet this has still not made me pick up 'Wuthering Heights' for my additional book club summer read. Well, ladies – you all know how I usually feel about the classics. But ... I have challenged myself this month and have tried some new things (e.g. painting and looking at photo enhancing software on the computer), my house is certainly better looked after, Daisy's had my full attention from the moment I wake up (no 'Wright Stuff' in the background when she's having her first play of the day) and Matt's probably had more of my attention in the evenings (though, hormonal as I am at the moment, I'm not sure he appreciates it). Would I do it again? Would I recommend it? Is my life enhanced? Two more days to find out.

Thursday 30th July

Even though this is the penultimate day of my challenge I have decided to make this my final diary entry for the month as I am already certain of the outcome of the experience. I have still not CONSCIOUSLY watched telly this month. Matt went out with friends tonight and I finished yet another novel. I wanted to order a Chinese takeaway till I realised I did not really want to sit and eat it myself without plonking myself down in front of the telly. Telly undoubtedly reduces the time people have to spend on perhaps more 'worthwhile' pursuits but for a great many people, myself included, it is also a great aid to relaxation and a 'comfort' after a stressful or tiring day and I, for one, will not be foregoing it any longer than necessary after tomorrow. So, the challenge has been a success. Have I learned anything? Well – yes! – Not to beat myself up about the things I do not manage to do – sometimes there are more important things to be doing – like relaxing. Finally, as far as work goes, the fact that I have had time and energy to plan lessons for the next six months in one of my subject areas – well, it's just not natural, is it?

Postscript

I forgot to mention Matt at the end. How did he do with this challenge? I don't think he even noticed the challenge was on and he continued in his non-telly watching ways as normal. I did however hear him in the living room with the telly on after we had stomped off to different rooms after an evening of grumping at each other. I can't remember what we were arguing about but I do remember lying in bed being rather tearful and feeling very sorry for myself. To be honest I'm not sure if my tears were brought on by our fight (whatever it was about) or because the lucky bugger was watching telly and I wasn't!

<u>*Further postscript*</u> *– added 1st August*

Matt gave me a long lie in bed this morning. Ate breakfast and then thought, as a special treat, I'd turn on the telly. Flicked through channels then switched off. Even though we have digital telly there was nothing I wanted to watch. I was tempted to watch an episode of 'Friends' for the umpteenth time before I mused on the challenge I had just undertaken and pulled myself up sharp. This, after all, is the kind of mindless telly watching I should be avoiding.

The same thing happened at night. My great plans for a Saturday night in front of the telly were put to rest when again I could not find anything I wanted to watch. Matt thought this would be an apt end to July's challenge. I'm sure he hopes this will be an area of my life which will be dramatically changed. What do I think? – Only time will tell.

Chapter 8 – August

Experimentation with Food

This is either to cook something we have never cooked before or try a food we have never eaten.

To many of you, this may seem like a kind of 'nothing' challenge, but to old stuck-in-a-food-rut me this is quite a nerve wracking challenge. I've always thought of myself as a fairly adventurous eater. When in France I'm happy to tuck into a plate of snails, frogs' legs or horse. In Italy I'll happily devour seafood pasta with the most amazing looking tentacles hanging off the plate. Even in restaurants at home I've bravely tried adrenal glands (forgotten what that's called just now … ah, yes, sweetbreads ... not yum!), pig's cheek or ostrich. But still Matt calls me unadventurous when it comes to eating. Why? Invariably (probably 99 times out of a hundred) I continue to order the same foods all the time, secure in the knowledge I will usually enjoy them. So, in Italian restaurants it's spaghetti carbonara or ham and mushroom pizza, in Indian restaurants it's Tandoori mixes, lamb madras or variations on the dish of butter chicken, in Spanish restaurants it's paella, meatball tapas or prawns in garlic and in Chinese restaurants it's chicken curry, beef in black bean sauce, crispy duck and deep fried won tons. Your first question to me may be how come I haven't dropped dead of a heart attack? I'll respond by saying that although my figure certainly gives away some of the tell tale signs of my eating habits, most of the time I actually have quite a good diet though with extremely generous portion sizes.

The challenge this month is therefore to try new foods at least once a day. This will hopefully most often be our evening meal made from a new and exciting recipe, but work, life, time and economics may curb our abilities in this area so I figure that if this is the case (or if we are eating out) then we should at least try something different for lunch, even if it is only varying the filling we try on our baguettes.

I'm thinking off the top of my head but here are some of the foods I've never even tried, usually because I think they look or sound gross or I don't know what to do with them; anchovies, capers, Marmite, Ovaltine, Vegemite, tripe (though thankfully, not whilst pregnant, I think), aubergines, fromage frais, pickles … I'm sure the list is endless but until I start looking at recipe books it's hard to think of foods you've never really heard of or tried – go on, have a go yourself.

N.B. The exception to the rule, as always is Daisy. We'll encourage her to try new foods when we think they're not too spicy but as our girl can (when she wants) be quite an adventurous wee eater we'll leave her to make her mind up on (after an initial taste) whether she likes a food or not.

Saturday 1st August

I've been thinking about my pregnancy nutrition and aware that I need to increase my fruit and vegetable consumption I've decided to start the month with a big, nutritious pot of vegetable soup. I've never really been a soup eater and have only ever made lentil or chicken and vegetable soup. Today I decided to make a creamed soup and although I should really have read a recipe book I thought I'd do my usual and 'experiment'. When buying ingredients I was unsure whether to buy cream, crème fraiche, soured cream or fromage frais.

I'm still not sure what the differences are so in the end I bought half fat single cream. I was also unsure whether you could pour cream into a stock. Would it curdle? Mix? Float on the top?

Success! I made a big pot of cream of leek and potato soup and it was lovely – well it was quite lovely and would have been even lovelier if I had added less pepper. I like my food highly spiced so duly ground lots of peppercorns with my mortar and pestle. Unfortunately my heavy hand ensured that Daisy could not eat any of the soup which is a real shame considering I was making it to a great extent for her. Lesson learned.

Sunday 2nd August

Unlike many of the challenges Matt started this one very keen to participate. We agreed yesterday that I'd start the challenge and he would take on his role today. As you know I suggested soup, so Matt has followed this by planning – soup (I don't actually make him follow in my footsteps – he just seems to want to!). Anyway today we had tomato, potato and garlic (lots and lots of garlic) soup. So although I may learn from yesterday's heavy hand with the pepper the same can not necessarily be said of Matt and the garlic press. However, the soup was "really good," as Daisy declared whilst screwing her face up into a little ball. I personally thought she was eating so she would be assured pudding but nevertheless it did Matt's confidence the world of good.

My turn again tomorrow – we won't necessarily take equal turns about as our schedules will vary throughout the month, but in the meantime having Matt make dinner is a real treat, for although he cooks occasionally he is reluctant to try anything new and I'm pretty sure that out of the perhaps ten meals he's made in the last year at least 8 of the times have been risotto. It's also quite exciting to hear him talking about wanting to try to make Myra's brilliant chocolate tart recipe. How new-man!

Monday 3rd August
Yum. Just finished dinner – Quiche Lorraine with pastry made from scratch (for the first time I can remember since Home Economics in Second Year at High School). I started by moaning about how long it took to rub in the pastry and decided that in future I'd but it ready made in the supermarkets, but I must say, I changed my mind when I tasted it. Matt agreed (he knows when to make the appropriate sounds but did at least seem genuine). Just as well, as to save time tomorrow I doubled up the pastry quantities and made a cheese and mushroom quiche for tomorrow. It looks kind of soggy as I didn't think to cook the mushrooms first, but tomorrow will tell. In any case it still smells a lot tastier than most of the vegetarian options I have made in the past.

Wednesday 5th August
Before I tell you today's yummy menu I'll reflect on the mushroom and cheese quiche. It was probably the nicest veggie dish I've ever made. It ended up being not too runny but not at all bulky. However, as a true carnivore I must say there was nothing there that wouldn't have been improved by a load of lovely smoked bacon. However - on to today's menu. It was Matt's turn today to do the cooking. He spent ages looking at cook books then in the afternoon went shopping for ingredients, even thinking about alternatives he could introduce when he was unable to

source some non-seasonal produce. For one of the few times ever I gave dinner, shopping or what was in the fridge no thought at all. Unfortunately just before 5 pm Matt found out about a Scottish Enterprise course starting this evening about starting your own business. I duly had minutes to think about what I could make for dinner. Lazy it may seem but I plumped for a 'snack-type' meal, which although I've eaten loads of times in cafes I've never 'cooked'. So, a tuna melt baguette it was and it was very nice. A meal – hardly, but at least I've still stuck to my challenge. All I can say is tomorrow's must be better!

Monday 10th August

It's been a few days since I last wrote. Excuse me whilst I loosen my belt! The past few days have been spent eating, not-drinking and general merrymaking. I'll give you a rundown of our culinary successes and failures. On Thursday, no doubt feeling rather guilty over the tuna melt cuisine Matt made a lovely dinner. It was a slightly changed jambalaya recipe. He had eaten jambalaya lots while he was in New Orleans but found a recipe in a pasta cookbook where the traditional rice had been substituted by pasta. It was absolutely gorgeous but again a rather too generous sprinkle of chilli had made it too well seasoned for Daisy which was a shame as she would have loved it. It had chicken, ham, tomatoes, lots of garlic, onions and chilli in with fusilli pasta. Matt recalls there also being more seafood in it when he ate it in New Orleans, but nevertheless, it was a big success, in my book.

On Friday we visited friends, Steph, Chris, Mary and Eric in their lovely new house in North Queensferry. Steph made lunch so the main course of courgette quiche counted as our new food for the day (lovely, but we're beginning to feel a little bit 'quiched-out'). In the evening I went to an art gallery show where I ran into a very glamorous woman I hadn't seen for ages. I told her I was pregnant and when later I commented about how she looked exactly the same since I had last seen her 10 years ago she looked me up and down and didn't say much but made a wee comment towards my pregnancy. She meant this entirely kindly but I wished I'd made a little more effort than getting up from my nap five minutes before I had to run out of the house.

On Saturday we had friends to stay with us in the country. I wanted to make Morag and Ben a sure-fire dinner as they keep raving about the venison I cooked for them last, so I made my fail-safe fillet steak with mushrooms and pepper sauce. I shouldn't say so myself but the thought of my fillet steak makes my mouth water even now. Matt surpassed himself with a lovely chocolate tart (our new meal for the day) although as time was running out for cooking he substituted homemade pastry for a shop bought sweet tart case.

I invited my dad for Sunday dinner and made a traditional roast beef dinner. I had already made macaroni cheese for our guests for lunch so this was the first time I was a bit stuck for time for making a new recipe. Tired and ready for my bed and so reluctant to fail a challenge, at nine o'clock at night I rustled up a batch of coffee kisses cakes. I made them with decaf coffee so the 'kick' wasn't quite there but they were OK nevertheless. I've never tasted them before so I don't really have anything to compare them with. They were slightly crunchy – are they meant to be?

So now you know why I'm loosening my belt. Eating cakes in bed at ten at night won't help but I can always pretend it's my pregnancy that's to blame. I've not yet put on any actual weight during the past 12 weeks (I must be burning up loads more calories for this to not have happened) but my shape is definitely turning more balloon-like. I'm sure the rest of this month will help this along.

Tuesday 11th August

Last night ended with another cook-a-thon. We had not really decided who was in charge of the challenge meal yesterday and by evening we still had not prepared anything. I had eaten at a café for lunch as I had spent most of the day in school preparing for the start of the year. When I got back at night I reheated the leftover roast beef for an easy dinner option. By 9 o'clock at night when we were starting to sit down to relax the last thing I wanted to think about was coming up with a new recipe which we could make from our store cupboard ingredients. Matt came to the rescue! He didn't tell me what he was making but needless to say when I went into the kitchen and saw him grinding rice with a pestle and mortar I was curious. The surprise ended up being 'Singin' Hinnys' or maybe that should be 'Hinnies', a fruit scone type mixture dry cooked on a griddle or frying pan. We ended up scoffing one each at about eleven o'clock at night in our bed. Verdict - OK but a bit heavy – no wonder the Scots race belted out so many great warriors of yesteryear.

Tonight we had a lovely meal – seems a bit unfair perhaps that I am saying that about the food I am cooking. I devised the recipe from thinking about a meal I sometimes have in a restaurant in Kelso. There I have chicken with brie and bacon with a mustard sauce, but as I am pregnant I substituted the brie for mozzarella. I've got to say it was not quite so good with my cheese but in making this I learned a new technique for making sauces. I looked up my Nick Nairn Cook School book and there was a recipe for a quick cream sauce where lemon juice is added to the cream as a thickening agent. This was a change from the usual way I'd have made a mustard sauce (as a white sauce with added mustard) and it was much better. I love that I may learn some new cooking techniques during this challenge but we must still try to be a bit more adventurous. I find it much easier buying ingredients in Edinburgh than in the Borders so, as we are spending the next few days in Edinburgh, hopefully our cooking can be a bit more inventive.

Wednesday 12th August

A fabulous day, personally and a yucky day, culinary-wise. We were at the hospital today for a nuchal scan which tells the probability that one or both of the twins would be born with Down's Syndrome. We had debated on whether to take the test a hundred times and were still in mixed frames of mind when we arrived at the hospital. The outcome of the tests would probably dictate whether we went on to have amniocentesis – riskier with twins than with singleton babies. Anyway we do not have to make that decision as, after measuring the folds at the back of the babies' necks we were told we are low risk. This is by no means a certainty – probably a 75-80% probability as a conservative estimate but it's certainly good enough for us and we're quite happy now to take our chances and are so, so relieve not to have to make any further decisions in the meantime.

On a culinary front once again we were left with virtually no time to shop or cook so I thought I'd try making a healthy option – a smoothie. You are probably sitting thinking this is not much of a challenge but before you scoff may I tell you it was a bloody disaster. I have no idea how smoothies are meant to be made but I whizzed up milk and blackberries in the liquidiser and the result was absolutely awful. Back to my cup of decaf tea and off to the shops tomorrow to but 'proper' healthy drinks – until I read a recipe for how to make my own version. Without a doubt this was the worst disaster yet as both Matt and I poured them down the sink, although I also chucked the remainder of the Singin' Hinnies and Coffee Kisses this morning so, all in all, we need to step up our efforts I think.

Friday 14th August

It's my last official weekday before I go back to school. I decided to step up my attempt at the challenge yesterday and made 2 new dishes. For dinner we had cowboy pie – not exactly haute cuisine but one of the teachers I work with mentioned she was making it for her sons and I thought it sounded rather lovely. It was. It consisted of corned beef and beans topped with mashed potato and cheese. Daisy loved it and is still talking about what cowboys eat! I followed this in the evening with a batch of blueberry muffins. These were such a success that I was in the kitchen at nine o'clock this morning making a batch of blueberry and blackberry muffins – how's that for keen? That has to be my new meal for today as we are spending most of today wandering around at the Edinburgh Festival. I've also just made some very yummy chicken and cashew nuts for lunch using some of the ingredients we bought yesterday at the Chinese supermarket. Matt had never eaten this before and he thought it was delicious. I used to make this many years ago so it can't count as my new meal for the day. It does make me reflect on the meals we all make in our pasts and wonder why we stop making them. Fashions and tastes change, I suppose or we become bored by or too used to certain recipes. There are many such recipes in my past that I have not cooked for years – beef bourguignon, stuffed mushrooms, crème caramel and crumbles amongst them. Now that I have just replanted rhubarb in the garden I suspect crumble may be about to return.

Sunday 16th August

We've just had a couple of days once again filled by food. Matt and I went out on Friday night after I had written my diary. Although we both felt we had been overdoing the food a tad we opted to go out for a meal. We had planned once again to walk about at the Edinburgh Festival but rain stopped play. We opted for a simple pizza and finished off with coffee and hot chocolate for me at our favourite café round the corner. How times have changed for us with my very pregnant hormones. Our date night was over by 7.30pm as I was practically falling asleep over my hot chocolate.

On Saturday afternoon we went to a children's birthday party at Edinburgh International Climbing Arena. The food was yummy and I managed to quietly pinch tons of untouched orange quarters once the kids had moved onto the cakes. On our return home I quickly made a pot of cream of mushroom soup using a selection of shitake, porcini, oyster and ordinary mushrooms. It was delicious and received the highest compliment from my dad when he commented, "it tastes even better than tinned soup".

We ate out with friends in the evening. The restaurants in town were all packed due to the Edinburgh Festival and although we were initially told we would only have our table for two hours we ended up being there for four (partly due to slow service and partly to great company). A great night started with cocktails (non-alcoholic for me) and finishing with chocolate orange ice cream – what a Saturday night!

Today was Matt's turn again for the cooking and we've just finished his first attempt at spaghetti carbonara. Bless him, he very carefully cooked off the eggy part of the recipe before adding the milk as he was being so careful with my pregnancy food orders. The result was a sticky but not very creamy sauce which tasted nice but was not really as it should have been. He also had to substitute cheddar for parmesan as the latter makes me feel sick at the moment so, all in all, I'm not really the ideal dinner guest at the moment.

I'm out tonight on a girly night in the Borders with three old friends from the village. I'm going to break the news to those who don't know that I'm pregnant – although the fact that I'm not drinking alcohol will no doubt alert them before I even open my mouth. I seem to be changing shape quite dramatically at the moment. Whether this is down to pregnancy or the eating habits of the past couple of weeks is anyone's guess. I should maybe stay away from baking books for the next week or two.

Wednesday 19th August

I started back at school on Monday for an in-service day. Matt stayed at home with Daisy and became a domestic god, tidying the house and making shortbread (his first attempt – verdict - pretty good). On Tuesday I was back to work proper. I'm teaching an infant class this year and was pleasantly surprised to start the day with no tears from parents or the children (or indeed myself considering how tired I'm feeling the moment). Daisy was back to nursery in the Borders so Matt had the opportunity to spend his time on job searching. We drove to Edinburgh at night as I had a night out with friends. Although I was looking forward to seeing my mates Morag, Steph and Sue, I was completely an utterly shattered and by 11pm was well and truly beginning to flag. Still, I managed to try my new food for the day – 2 courses in fact and ordered smoked fish chowder and then linguine with a garlic and wild mushroom sauce. It would have been lovely but the smell of parmesan at the moment is turning my stomach – not really a good recommendation for any restaurant so I won't name it as they are completely blameless for my hormonal reactions. I'll just continue to take them out on poor Matty instead!

I'm just about to go into the kitchen now to start preparing tonight's dinner. Kung – po chicken, using ingredients we bought last week from the Chinese supermarket. A bit of a cheat really as I'm using some of their paste or sauce (not sure till I open it as I can't read the Chinese writing but am using all the authentic accompanying vegetables. Must go now, as salivating on the laptop probably isn't the safest thing to do.

Saturday 22nd August

Once again I have to do a bit of a catch up of my diary as life has been so hectic. Being back at work isn't half interrupting my hobbies! The kung po chicken last week was good but nothing compared to the meal Matt made on the Thursday night. He cooked chicken in a cream, garlic and onion sauce with tagliatelle and it was absolutely fantastic. This will definitely be one of our dinner party menus for the future. Yesterday and today's efforts from me have been pathetic. Yesterday (in a café) I had a treacle scone as I'd never eaten one before. Verdict – OK and I may have it again although

I'd sooner stick to my fruit scones. Today was even worse. I cooked … wait for the excitement … cabbage! I'd never cooked it before and although I thought it was lovely it was probably helped by the super large knob of butter I added at the end. I cut it into shreds and steamed it for a couple of minutes till it had wilted – was that what I was supposed to do with it – who knows (well, probably millions of people know actually). As I felt particularly lazy I thought I'd add in a new food (just a few minutes ago as it happens). I made a slice of toast and spread it with … Marmite (please don't write in for the recipe – I am far too busy at the moment). Verdict – gag – straight to bucket. I'm so shocked. I expected to love it (I'd only recently been told it was salty and like Oxo cubes) as I love Twiglets so much. Yeeeeeeeeeeeeeeeeeeeeeeeeeuck!

Sunday 23rd August

As always when I've just had a day or two of sloth and haven't felt like I've been making an adequate effort at my challenges, I have spent the day overcompensating like mad. Today so far …. And I may not have finished yet; I have made chicken noodle soup, cherry muffins and prune and raisin muffins. All this after a swim too – Health Central here just now. We have been discussing our diet more since this challenge began and Matt and I have decided to try to cut the giant bag size of Cadbury's buttons and Maltesers we tend to buy a few times each week (and Daisy doesn't even get to see them). We're also really starting to come to terms with having twins and are now getting rather excited about it. Yesterday we tried out car seats in our Citroen and there's no way we'll be able to fit three in easily (although we had managed to find a buggy which would fit in the boot) so it's off to car search we go. So … new car, buy car seats, buy double buggy, cook a new food every day, Matt unemployed, I start tomorrow working every Monday between 2 different schools … no pressure then!

Wednesday 26th August

I came home from a tiring day at work on Monday to a newly bakes batch of chocolate chip and orange cookies. They tasted good but had been rolled to almost an inch thick. I think Matt could have made 3 times the amount if they'd been made as intended (do you notice a slight tired crabbiness to my voice here?). Nevertheless, I'm impressed with my new man's ability to embrace his inner baker. On Tuesday Matt was out on a stag night and for the first time in ages I could not be bothered thinking about food. I never thought I'd see the day that I wanted nothing more than a plain baked tattie every night but that day is definitely arriving. On Tuesday therefore I took another easy option and for the first time ever cooked (well, heated) mackerel covered in cracked black pepper. I'd never eaten mackerel before and am aware I should be trying to eat more oily fish so that was the reasoning behind my purchase. It was lovely but the amount of bones did put me off somewhat. Today I took another easy option and with readymade pasta made herb and garlic tortellini with a crème fraiche, cheese and pepper sauce (shop bought and not to my taste but enjoyed by both Matt and Daisy). The next couple of days will be hard. I'm teaching and looking after Daisy on my own and have plans for both evenings so I'm going to have to think of some very easy cooking options ('Really?' I can almost hear you say aloud).

Friday 28th August

Yesterday's challenge food sounds pathetic in theory but in practice it turned out to be the most difficult to make yet. Wait for it – popcorn. I bought corn from a health food shop rather than the microwaveable packets from the supermarket. On my first attempt (I warned you) I heated it in a pan on the stove until ready … well not exactly ready but half of the kernels popped the other half burnt and yucky. On my second attempt I used the microwave. I wanted to pop all the kernels obviously so left them in for ages until … I almost set fire to the mass, I melted the bottom of the plastic dish and I cracked Daisy's favourite plastic plate in two. This 'glob' continued to smoke for several minutes even when left on my garden path to cool. On my third attempt in the microwave I gave up when about half the kernels had popped and used a sieve to separate the two different 'masses'. I poured maple syrup over the useable ones – lovely. How I love an easy supper snack! I want into work today and asked other staff how you should do it – shake the pan apparently – we live and learn.

Today I phoned Matt at lunchtime and asked him, as we had a wedding to go to tonight, if he could rustle up something different as a snack for before or after the wedding. When I got home there was a huge tray of raisin and chocolate fudge in the fridge. I don't like fudge normally but this was yummy (as it should be with 350 grams of good quality chocolate). We're going to dinner with friends tomorrow so I detect a lovely home-made present may be winging their way.

Sunday 30th August

Another hectic day yesterday. We all started the day quite tired after a late night at my cousin George and his new wife Marion's wedding. It was a lovely night and we managed to extract Daisy at ten o'clock before she got to the grumpy stage (how lovely only to hear good comments about your child's behaviour). In the afternoon we went to a birthday party for one of Daisy's wee mates in Edinburgh then drove straight down to the Borders to have dinner at our friends Mary and Sean's house. For an easy relaxed night with a chance to have a good old catch up we had agreed it'd be a good idea to order in a take-away. Now, if I had been thinking straight I would have asked for something I hadn't eaten before. I didn't. Instead, after getting home at half past ten I had to go straight to the kitchen to start cooking. How dedicated am I or should I ask 'how bad a loser am I'? Anyway 12 coffee and walnut muffins later we retired to bed for another wee supper snack. It's a good job I'm pregnant because I don't think I could justify my eating habits any other way the moment.

Today we had a lunch we had never tried before – Cajun chicken pizza, but as this was ready-made and it's the weekend I thought I'd better step up my game a bit so after the huge roast beef dinner I'm making for friends and family tonight we're having apple and plum crumble (apples from dad's garden, plums from Mary and Sean's garden). I've even made a spare for dad to take home. I can now relax for the month as that's all my thinking about food done (for the next day anyway) as Matt has promised to end the month's challenge with a good 'un.

Monday 31st August

Matt did us proud. For his finale he made fish pie with mushrooms, topped with thinly sliced potatoes. He was so proud, bless him, I hardly commented on the fact

111

that the mushrooms had made the cream sauce like thin soup and the tatties would have, in my opinion, been much better mashed. Still, we finished the meal with some more of his home made chocolate and raisin fudge, so I've got so hand it to him the boy did good!

Postscript

Has this month's challenge changed anything? Well, it's only the start of September as I write this, but I think it has. Matt has cooked more for me in the past month than he has altogether in the 7 years we've been together. What's more, he has been extremely adventurous in his food choices. I, too, seem to have broken out of my rut, although I've really missed some of my curries which were a fairly staple part of our diet. We're having friends to dinner at the weekend and normally serving vegetarian food presents us with a dilemma as to what to cook. No longer. I'm planning to rustle up some quiches, but even if we didn't fancy that I'd be much more inclined to try something new. I've also just made a quick pot of soup for lunch entirely from leftovers. As we had cream left over from last night's dinner this seemed like a rich and delicious lunch treat. I fully intend to try to make the most of leftover and unused food we have in the house and will happily accept any surplus fruit and veg friends and neighbours have in their gardens. Pies and crumbles will no doubt be filling our freezer soon instead of our bucket receiving any fruit and veg which was bought in excess or started to turn bad. Might not make you salivate at the thought but our different challenges seem to be amalgamating...

Just so you can see the effort or lack-of-effort we have made this month here it is, below (actually the food choices don't seem too bad when I see it in print – the fact that I am a compulsive list maker does however alarm me):

1st   Leek and potato soup - Jackie

2nd   Tomato, potato and garlic soup - Matt

3rd   Quiche Lorraine - Jackie

4th   Cheese and mushroom quiche - Jackie

5th   Tuna melt baguette - Jackie

6th   Jambalaya with pasta - Matt

7th   Courgette quiche - friend

8th   Chocolate tart - Matt

9th   Coffee kisses - Jackie

10th   Singin' Hinnies - Matt

11th   Chicken with mozzarella and bacon in a mustard sauce - Jackie

12th   Smoothie - Jackie

13th   Cowboy pie and blueberry muffins - Jackie

14th   Blueberry and blackcurrant muffins - Jackie

15th   Cream of mushroom soup - Jackie

16th   Spaghetti carbonara - Matt

17th   Shortbread - Matt

18th   Smoked fish chowder, linguine with wild mushroom and garlic sauce -   restaurant

19th   Kung po chicken - Jackie

20th   Chicken in a cream, onion and garlic sauce with tagliatelle - Matt

21s   Treacle scone - cafe

22nd   Cabbage and marmite on toast – Jackie (though Matt made himself a slice later too)

23rd   Chicken noodle soup, cherry muffins and prune and raisin muffins - Jackie

24th   Chocolate chip and orange cookies - Matt

25th   Mackerel – Jackie (all the effort, putting them under the grill)

26th   Garlic and herb tortellini with crème fraiche, cheese and pepper sauce – even I'm not taking credit for heating up these ready meal tubs and packets

27th   Popcorn with maple syrup – Jackie (and I still can't get rid of the smell of burning)

28th   Chocolate and raisin fudge - Matt

29th   Coffee and walnut muffins - Jackie

30th   Cajun chicken pizza, plum and apple crumble – Jackie (for heating and actual cooking)

31st   Fish pie – Matt

Chapter 9 – September

Competitions

I.e. Entering as many competitions as possible in a month.

This may seem like a really strange challenge. Why is it a challenge at all you may ask? Well, the reasoning behind this challenge is as follows:

- Apart from our wonderful impending babies news I feel like we've had a hard few months both emotionally and financially.
- Matt is still unemployed.
- I met someone years ago who gave up a good job to enter competitions full time. He had won cars, holidays, tellies and I think a house (though my memory may have enlarged that 'fact' or 'fiction'). He claimed his success was down to great slogan writing.
- I have a friend whose friend won a car, a holiday to America and a holiday to Canada. She claimed her success was down to the sheer quantity of competitions she entered.
- We could do with cheering up.
- This challenge doesn't seem quite as difficult as many of the recent ones and I'm still absolutely shattered.
- A windfall of lots of baby stuff would be brilliant.
- A windfall of any stuff would be lovely – we shall see – I may win lots of 50p off vouchers.

Tuesday 1ˢᵗ September

Day One. Not really sure where to start with this but I have tentatively made some rules I intend to follow:

- I will not go in for any competitions I have to pay to enter
- I will not go in for competitions in which I would not be able to use the prize (e.g. tickets to a music festival would be no good to me right now considering I need to use the toilets every few minutes)
- Although I wrote I'd enter as many competitions as possible in a month I've decided to put a time limit on it of about an hour a day (I still have a job, family and life after all … though wouldn't this be a nice alternative future career, sitting in my lovely home in France entering competitions all day?)

I started my search tonight on the internet and entered the following questions:

From the 'Heat' magazine website –
Which of the colours was the title of a Daniel Merriweather single?
Answer – Red
Prize – tickets to see him at the Shepherd's Bush Empire in London and an overnight stay in a hotel.
I've never heard of him but quite fancy a night in London. The answer was in the blurb next to the competition.

Also on 'Heat' website –
How many blades does the new Gillette Venus Embrace have?
Answer – 5
Prize – yes, you've guessed it – a razor

The answer to this was on the advertisement. I thought the chances of winning may be quite good as this is such a cheap prize – there must be hundreds to give away.

'Orange' phone competition from their website
This involved filling out a personality profile called 'This is who I am', whereby I will probably be inundated with offers from different companies. I am, however, entered into a draw for loads of prizes.

From 'Grazia' magazine website
What is "The 54" based on?
Answer – Studio 54
Prize – a £480 Freda sequin jacket
I have no idea what a Freda jacket is but I knew the answer to this one

Also from 'Grazia' website
In which city does Alexander McQueen show?
Answer – Paris
Prize – A £160 Alexander McQueen scarf
The answer to this one was on the website. I thought the £160 scarf would look good with my £40 outfit!

Also from 'Grazia' website
Which British actress appears on the cover of Sept 2007 issue of American Vogue?
Answer – Sienna Miller (I think – answer not given anywhere but I think I've seen a picture of her with Anna Wintour promoting the film)
Prize – Tickets to the aforementioned film, 'The September Issue' and £150 to spend at Oasis (will go nicely with my dead-expensive scarf).

Yet again from 'Grazia' website

What is Vivienne Westwood notorious for (multiple choice)?

Answer – not wearing knickers (again, I think – vaguely remember scandal sheet stuff about this in the past)

Prize - £100 Vivienne Westwood fragrance set

From the 'Telegraph' newspaper website

Simply, entering personal details for a chance to win a weekend for 2 at a luxury art filled hotel.

Also from the 'Telegraph' website

This time entering personal details and filling out a short questionnaire for a chance to win dinner for 2 at Gordon Ramsay's restaurant at Claridges or, as this is in association with 'Gordon's' a bottle of gin

It'll be nice to have a restaurant to pop along to when we've been to Daniel Whatshisname's concert.

Total amount of competitions entered today – 9.

It's now 11pm at night and Matt has just let me back on MY laptop as he has spent the last hour and a half entering competitions. Unlike me, who occasionally thought about lovely prizes that we could share such as hotel breaks or fabulous meals, Matt has entered to win the following prizes;

An Enermax PSU from 'Custom PC', TV speakers from 'Focus', Kaspersky from 'PC Answers', Norton anti-virus from 'PC Format', Paintshop Pro and USB storage from 'What Laptop', £300 worth of Maxgear from 'MBR' (a bike magazine) and, strangely, a mattress from 'Homes and Antiques'. I'm finding his reading or research matter a bit strange and have probably spelled most of the prizes wrongly as I've not heard of many of them.

I've also decided that as it's taken me ages to type up my diary tonight with so much detail, from now on I'm only going to list the prizes we've gone for and where they're from. So, to add to my tally of 9, Matt has added another 8, therefore today we have entered 17 competitions.

Wednesday 2nd September

My goodness, this challenge is addictive and totally intoxicating at the thought of all the wonderful prizes we could win. Yesterday I had a hard time getting Matt off the computer and today he broke the rules about not spending money and bought a 'Take a Break' magazine for 78p for the competitions. I do not approve and told him so. For one thing the magazine contains horrible tabloid tales which I could not bear to read and furthermore I'm disturbed that he's even heard of the magazine, let alone has thought to buy it. Anyway, I've asked him not to spend any more on competitions and have said I'll deduct the 78p from the value of any prizes we win. Can you imagine what it is like to live with me? Please don't answer this to my face.

Today I have entered 26 competitions for the following prizes:

A Henry Holland tee-shirt and 5 pair of tights (I agree, who?), a £1330 handbag, a Mamas and Papas pushchair, £200 worth of VTech baby gear, a Spa break in Cardiff, a Hauck pushchair, a Mamas and Papas activity cradle, a Clippasafe home safety pack, an interactive toy from Lamaze, a Fisher Price toddler toy, nursery accessories, a £490 travel system, 1 year's supply of Comfort Pure, 1 month's supply of Huggie's nappies and wipes, 1 year's supply of Andrex Kids and a selection of Tomy Discovery prizes, Pop It, Rock It

119

CD, Halos N Horns bath time treats, Day by Day Pregnancy book, VTech baby monitor, Tippitoes Girl about Town bag, a Fisher Price Dwell studio bouncer, a Bliss 'Going home Pack', a Morrck baby hoodie, £600 worth of beauty products, £350 worth of Weleda's skincare products and a double buggy… and I'd happily settle for a fraction of that!

Thursday 3rd September
My addiction continues. I'm in the Borders tonight without broadband so can't do any searching for competitions so I spent my lunch break today at a friend's house searching the internet and managed to enter 8 altogether. These were for the following: a Mothercare 'My Choice' pushchair, a weekend for 4 at Legoland, 9 month's supply of pomegranate juice, a safety gate, Mothercare, Fairy and Pamper prizes, a £200 gift voucher for an 'experience', a designer handbag and £100 worth of Soap and Glory products.

As yet I've obviously no idea if this will be a complete waste of time or not, but (dreams…) if we win only a couple of prizes this has to be worth spending at least half an hour a day. It'd be like doing the premium bonds, only possibly with slightly better odds. I'm so excited. I feel like the way I did hundreds of years ago when my dad let me pick the teams for his football pools. I was so convinced we would win that I had already spent the prize money in my head. Of course the fact that I wanted to buy a monkey and a dodgem car might give away my age at the time (I was 26). But, just imagine ….

Friday 4th September
Boy, do I know how to have fun on a Friday night? I've been sitting at the computer for 2 hours solid (it's now

9.45pm) answering competitions and even as I started to list what these were I decided this month's reading was becoming too boring for words so I've decided that from now on I will only tell you about how many I have entered.

So, in total, tonight I entered a staggering 68 competitions.

I'm amazed – when I started this I hoped to enter a hundred competitions in a month. Now I find I've managed to do that in 4 days. Surely there must be some return on this.

Sunday 6th September

I didn't manage any competitions yesterday as we had friends over for most of the day and by evening I was too wiped to sit in front of the computer. Matt, however, managed to enter 11 competitions on Friday night and 6 yesterday morning. I have just spent an hour and a quarter entering 27 competitions.

(Total so far this month between us – 163 competitions)

Tuesday 8th September

Over the last couple of days I've been furiously trying to enter competitions but it's starting to get a bit harder. I've already picked most of the 'biggie' magazines and the last few I've tried have been extremely time consuming to enter. I've also made a lot of guesses today to competition questions rather than spend extra time on research. Today we also spend ages in a garage looking for a different (much bigger) car. They're bringing one in for us to see on Saturday and as I have no interest in cars I pretty much expect to buy it regardless (as long as it will fit our ever expanding brood). Although I haggled the price in advance and reduced it by £500 I came away thinking I should have tried for more. Matt's going to try again on Saturday but I'll just keep telling myself that I'll make it all back soon on my competition wins.

My ongoing tally is that I entered 55 competitions between yesterday and today.

Total so far – 218 competitions (Secretly I'm now aiming for 500 in the month but I'm not sure this will be at all possible).

Wednesday 9th September

Today I've been hitting the wedding magazines and I'm astonished. I've always thought I was missing the bride gene and have never shown any interest in getting married or having a big wedding, but when I started looking at some of the wedding venues I got almost teary eyed – could be the fact that I am pregnant with a way too much sticking out belly for this stage. Anyway today I entered in total 40 competitions and I have lots of scope left for many more bridal competitions.

Total so far – 258 competitions (half way there to my revised target)

Saturday 12th September

Oh my goodness – how things have changed. It's getting so much harder now to enter competitions. I've been through all the magazines I can think of and have now covered many of the newspapers as well and although I've been at the computer for ages today I've only managed 11 competitions. I completed 17 last night by finishing looking at all the wedding magazines. I'm not really sure what my next tack should be – do I start looking at magazines where I have little ideas of the answers e.g. cars or computer magazines? I'm going to sleep on it and will let you know tomorrow. I may start researching big department stores and supermarket chains – they're bound to have some competition surely. Watch this space – I'm hoping inspiration will strike overnight but I'm starting to worry about my 500 competition target.

Total so far – 286 competitions

Sunday 13th September

I've worked out how to do it. Today Matt has entered the same competitions that I've already entered. This was much, much easier than the first time around as I have already done the research into the answers and can simply tell him if he's stuck on any. Anyway, through this wee brainwave there were a total of 49 competitions entered today taking **the overall total to 335.**

Monday 14th September

Phew – I'm exhausted. A tiring day at work today, not eased by 3 hours driving from and to Edinburgh meeting road works all along the way. However as soon as I got home tonight I sat at the computer for another 2 hours and 45 competitions later (repeats of ones I've done but this time Matt entering again) I'm ready for a good old slump in front of the telly. I had also heard about a competition with the prize of a free wedding at the Roxburgh Hotel just outside of Kelso and as that is my favourite place to get away to I phoned to find out more details. It seems you have to attend a wedding fair there to qualify for entry and even though a) we've no immediate plans to marry and b) it's outside of competition month, I think we'll be going. What a prize after all.

I've also decided the next tactic I'm going to take – I'm going to enter all the computer competitions in the hope I can win a prize for Matty and then it's onto car magazines … I'll just have to hope none of the competitions require any specialist knowledge.

Overall total now 380 competitions.

Tuesday 15th September

A mega-successful day today. Matt started by telling me that he had entered 10 competitions from his 'Take a Break' magazine he had bought a couple of weeks ago. I asked him for the answers so I could enter them too and he said it was too late because the competitions had now closed. So much for share and share alike, the bugger! He wanted to go and buy the next copy of the magazine but I've told him not to this month as he had already broken the rules (well, my rules) by doing so - having said that, I was obviously prepared to break them too, if I'd been in time to enter the competitions. Do you think living with me might be a tad harsh at times? I don't think I'm going to come off too well in this book somehow.

Tonight I babysat for our friends Sue and Alex and I spent much of the night on their computer entering more competitions. It was a struggle – they have a Mac which I don't really know how to use so I was working really slowly in case I pressed a button which made the screen disappear or minimize or, well, anything really. Overall today then I have managed to enter another 40 competitions and so far I've still not had to go for car or computer ones. I had a brainwave this morning and thought about all the food magazines that are out there so that's what I've been concentrating on today. Tomorrow I'm going to have a go with the diet and fitness magazines – I'll just have to hope I can postpone any prizes I win there for quite a while (see, ever the optimist).

By the way, today I kept getting missed calls on my mobile phone with a number I didn't recognise. It could be the start of junk phone calls with all the competitions I've been entering (though I have been ticking the boxes for no calls) or … I may have won something. With this in mind I have kept my mobile at the side of me all night.

Total now 430

Wednesday 16th September

Daisy was at nursery this afternoon and I have now done an embarrassing amount of competitions. The slimming magazines turned out to be duds but I got on to some really good TV listing magazines and supermarket chain magazines and today, I'm almost embarrassed to say I completed 66 competitions bringing my total now to **496.**

Since my revised target was 500 I figure I'm nearly there. My obsessive character has meant that I spent much of today working on competitions instead of relaxing with a good book or the telly, so from now on I'm going to limit myself ABSOLUTELY to one hour a day. I was talking to my pal Morag today and was pondering the fact that if I'd bought 500 lottery tickets I'd be astonished if I didn't win a prize so I figure that should be plenty to give me a chance in competitions. So, next question – can I trust myself to limit my newest temporary addiction?

Thursday 17th September

I'm very proud to say I have spent about half an hour on the computer tonight, have been looking at gardening sites and have entered 14 competitions and NOW I'M GOING TO STOP. DID YOU HEAR

THAT? Of course it could be because I've already played Scrabble with my dad for a tenner, have won and am now absolutely shattered. Really, I don't know how an 18 week pregnant old lady is meant to teach all day, play Scrabble for ages at night and then be expected to enter more than 14 competitions. Matt, bless him is putting Daisy to bed and I'm going to pour a cuppa, put my feet up and watch Masterchef.

Total … 510 (WOW!)

Monday 21st September

I have, contrary to my obsessive compulsive usual behaviour, been taking it easy over the weekend but have managed to find a couple of really good sites for competitions – all gardening, so the tally is as follows. On Friday I did 13 competitions, bringing the total to 523. On Saturday I did 24 – a total of 547 and on Sunday I did 18 making a grand total of 565. When I looked on at Matt last night, working away assiduously on his computer I assumed he was hard at work on business 'things' but he too was entering loads of competitions. As I was asleep when he came to bed I have no idea how many he has entered but I will update you later tonight.

Later … Matt completed 9 competitions last night and tonight, although I have been on the internet for ages, I have only managed to find and complete 5 competitions. **Our total is now 579 competitions.**

Tuesday 22nd September

This is starting to become really difficult. I have to search for a long time to find competitions I want to enter. There are certainly competitions I could enter but the main question just now is really 'do I want the prizes?' I started looking through hobby magazines online and came upon competitions in a knitting magazine, but almost all the prizes were for yarn. As I can barely knit a square and don't even enjoy knitting that I thought it best to leave these ones alone. Tonight I managed to find some competitions from bookshops – my favourite type of shops in the world so I'm quite excited about those. As for Matt, well the little star has just gone and got his first job as a self employed person so he's busy beavering away on the laptop – I'm so proud of him. The job doesn't involve much money at all, will only take him a day, but it's the most exciting bit of money that's came into this house in a long time. A start at last to our new future as entrepreneurs, or should I say entrepreneur and hanger-on?

Total now – after another 16 today – **595 competitions.**

Thursday 24th September

After a break yesterday from competition entering (due to extreme tiredness) I was pleasantly surprised today to find lots of new competitions to enter. This is due to some of the magazines I have already found having their next issue out, complete with lots of new lovely prizes to win. I am slightly concerned, however, that I still have not heard about any of the previous competitions I have entered. Does this mean anything or do they take ages in their replies? … Time will tell. I am becoming more and more aware of why companies give out good prizes in their competitions though. Today I came across a new multi child car seat which would perhaps be suitable for fitting our upcoming three children into our little Citroen. I'm going to check out the website tonight but am already convinced that if I do not win one then I might quickly be purchasing thereafter. I would never even have heard of this product unless it had been a prize, so I can see where the benefits are from companies and magazines which can attract new readers or competitors. In total I entered 23 competitions today bringing us to a **grand total of 618.**

Sunday 27th September
On Friday I managed again to revisit some of the sites I had used before which now had a new group of competitions displayed. I added another 14 to my total. By yesterday I was beginning to struggle again, however, so in desperation I again joined a competition website. This one seems slightly better than the last I looked at. The competitions are displayed clearly, they can be searched for by category or prize value and they tell you how many people have entered from their website compared to how many prizes are on offer. The only thing most of the prize givers want you to do is to log in or sign onto their website and I figure there is so little time in the month I can always unsubscribe in a few days. So far I have just looked at the categories of beauty, food and books but between today and yesterday I answered another 21 competitions.
My grand total is now 653 competitions.

Wednesday 30th September
Well, it's now the end of the month and it's ending, not on a bang, but a fizzle. I am now finding it extremely tiring (either the pregnancy or the competition entering) and have definitely taken the easy road towards the end of the month. I entered 5 competitions yesterday, all individual entries to new competitions I found, as I am not completely convinced by the competition websites – I think I may be inundated with mail by them and

don't want to have to spend too long extricating myself from their mailing lists.

The grand total is therefore at the end of the month – 658 competitions.

So far I've won NOTHING. Many of the competitions, indeed most of them, are still to reach a closing date. Am I dismayed? To be honest – yes! I hoped by now there would be some kind of return on my efforts. Will I enter any more? Yes, there are some magazines in particular which make competition entering very easy and which offer incredible prizes. I intend to keep going with the baby and bride magazines for the next wee while at least until either the notion of becoming a bride or the reality of motherhood without the latest gadgets sets in.

Bet you can't wait for the update? Will I be a mega-winner? Wait and see.

Chapter 10 – October

Putting the Thought Back into Christmas

Deciding on the challenges for each month is becoming more and more difficult as my pregnancy advances. At 5 months pregnant I am certainly becoming less physically and emotionally able to take on some challenges than others. I had been toying with a month of vegetarianism again (as I am such a carnivore) and although I am eating a lot less meat (due to the fact that I cannot have it cooked rare) I just can't force myself to restrict my diet any more than it has been already.

So back to this month – whilst I am still able to get around the shops if needed (though at the moment I am lying with my leg up in bed due to a very sore knee – hopefully not the start of the knee problems I had with Daisy which resulted in my need for crutches and a wheelchair for ages before and after the birth) I have decided to make this the month that I will be trying to put thought and not necessarily money into Christmas.

Times for Matt and I, like many others, are pretty tough financially at the moment. Matt still has not found work two and a half months on from his redundancy, but odd jobs for his role as self employed consultant are beginning to trickle in (well the second small job just arrived yesterday). Although we are normally major Christmas celebrators we're going to restrict our present buying to around £50 each for both Xmas and birthdays and will really cut down on the amount we'll buy Daisy.

The aim for this month therefore is to try to make this Christmas special and festive without breaking the bank or going into any debt and to instead put the time and effort into finding thoughtful gifts for family and friends.

Saturday 10th October

I'm starting this month's diary much later than usual as there is not much at all to report … except … wait for it … my first (note I say first) competition prize has come through. It's a book about bugs from Dorling Kindersley and although it hardly sets my world on fire I am incredibly happy at winning anything (which has been looking increasingly unlikely).

As for the Xmas ideas – I have spent loads of time thinking about and planning some ideas for Daisy, Matt and my dad and have even bought a few cheap trinkets which I aim to use in my Xmas gifts.

I've been trawling through our family photos and have so far made a collection of all the photos of Daisy and my dad and all the photos of Daisy and Matt. I'm planning to make special memory books for both Matt and my dad or perhaps collages of some kind, but rather than rush ahead I'll see what I can come up with over the next few weeks.

I've asked the nursery at my school for the recipe for little Xmas cakes so I think Daisy and I may be really busy on that front next month. With that in mind I have started collecting little tins to bake them in (little bean or sweet corn- type cans).

As for Daisy – she occasionally watches Channel 5 in the mornings for the cartoons and unlike CBeebies this means adverts. So far she apparently wants every toy which has been invented with perhaps the exception of a few 'boy' toys. She also reiterated this fact with a recent visit to Toys "R" Us. I very nearly fell into the usual Xmas trap there too. As we walked around the lanes with Daisy pointing out every piece of pink plastic crap as her dearest desire, I started counting up how much it was going to cost. Luckily I didn't impulse buy and by the time I had got home I realised that NO thought at all would have went into that particular shop.

I am very aware that my one to one time with Daisy is limited so with this in mind I want to make the majority of her Xmas goodies things she can experience with Matt or myself. I'm planning to buy her a fabric calendar which we can spend time doing every day (how teacher-ish) but will also aim for fun with a really good set of face paints, assuring her time with mummy and daddy. I'm sure I too will cave and will buy her some total junk that she 'really needs', but so far I've resisted buying anything at all for her.

For friends I'm hoping to make thoughtful gifts by buying funky frames for pictures of their children, making homemade sweets in December or by customising T shirts etc with fabric paints and pens. I'm also planning a trip soon to a ceramic painting workshop with Daisy for personal handmade gifts for her daddy and granddad.

I wouldn't imagine I'd be keeping this diary as vigilantly this month as I certainly don't imaging I'll have ideas or make/ buy gifts every day, but I'm cutting myself some slack since I'm also going to be starting my pregnancy and baby books for my impending SON AND DAUGHTER (just found out on Wednesday). I went out to buy them a book before realising that they're not going to be the 'twins' to me forever but two actual beings who need their own book each. Again, just starting to sink in!

Tuesday 13th October

A round of applause please. Today I managed to complete all the Xmas present buying for Daisy including a present from my dad to her (he knows nothing about it yet but always asks what he should buy her – this year it's an animatronic Dalmatian). As for our presents to Daisy – beware, they are pretty educational – the first thing I bought today was the fabric wall hanging calendar which I've got in my classroom and which Daisy is always asking for. Whilst I was in the shop I bartered the guy down by £10 by agreeing to also buy a fabric reward chart for tasks undertaken in the house. I plan to give this to Daisy when she has her brother and sister as many of the rewards are things like a trip to the cinema or special treat time with mum or dad which I think she'll really need and love. I've also ordered the face paints I was thinking about. On my shopping trip today I spotted a great educational game/toy which took both Matt and I back to our childhoods. It's a lacing kit where shoe laces (well coloured lovely looking laces) are laced through a picture. It's designed to improve fine motor skills (teacher talking again) but, more than that, I think Daisy will love doing it and it'll keep her occupied for ages. I also ordered three books online about a little girl called Daisy which were recommended to me by one of the mums at my school and they look great. Her stocking will only hold a few sweeties, fruit and thoughtful little tokens so I started the ball rolling by buying a wee bauble, a snow globe with her name inside. There is no point in buying the yummies as we're far too likely to eat them long before Xmas. Finally, just so you know we intend Xmas to be fun as well as educational (yawn) I caved and bought her a talking Minnie Mouse and a set of sparkly dressing up shoes. Money dependent – I've also said to Matt that if we have some spare she'd love a Minnie Mouse dress up costume. So – a job well done – if I go into labour far too early that is one load of presents I do not have to think about.

Friday 16th October

Sleigh bells ring … I'm getting into the Christmas mood. Daisy and I spent a couple of hours yesterday at one of the ceramic painting workshops decorating a coffee cup and saucer for Matt's Christmas. It still has to be glazed but I can collect it from tomorrow onwards. I can't wait to see it. I admit I did a lot of the decoration myself BUT Daisy helped to do the initial base coat of paint, wrote her name over dots I had made (which I then went over in paint) and made handprints on it with the help of Cindy, the lovely lady who runs the shop. It was a great, relaxing experience, helped to a great extent by the integral soft play area, selection of lovely glossy magazines and coffee shop. I'd love to do this more often but, with our financial situation, it'll have to be an occasional treat.

On a less expensive but equally creative note I got lots of copies of photos of my dad and Daisy over the past 3 years and have made up a little Grandad's Boasting Book. It looks pretty good but still needs a bit of time and effort put in to personalise it more. Matt's book, on the other hand, is now complete and looks absolutely wonderful. I started with a lovely wee photograph album and overall it took about 150 photos (most of which are tiny passport size) to complete. So, although it is a book of wee photos, I've aimed to make it a treasury of big memories. I'm absolutely over the moon with it and bought a silver pen today to inscribe it with lovely messages – I have no doubt my big soft man will shed a tear or two when he opens it on Christmas morning.

Photographs seem to me to be a fantastic way to make thoughtful Christmas gifts. I've been experimenting with Photo shop software and am now more competent at cropping and fixing any faults on my photographs, so am giving lovely photos in frames to several people for Christmas. I'm feeling very 'Blue Peter' at the moment so am off to eat a snack I made earlier!

Friday 23rd October

This month has been quite shocking as far as diary entries goes. I feel I've hardly written anything mainly because there's not too much to report. Daisy's presents are now wrapped and complete. I've been back to the ceramic workshop with Daisy and have made a mug for her grandad. We plan to make another couple of pieces before Xmas for my Auntie Evelyn and cousin Christine, both of whom are planning to spend Xmas day with Matt, Daisy, dad and I.

I've finished my dad's Xmas. He's constantly thinking about entrepreneurial ways to make some money just now, so to go along with sweeties and DVDs, I've bought him a very simple book on how to create your own website as I think he'd find this quite a good challenge.

I've had no further ideas for Matt apart from the photo album and mug we've made for him. I'm not going to rush to buy something but am going to wait, hopefully, for inspiration to strike.

As for everyone else – well I've been busy but can't complete most of the presents this month. I've been going round the charity shops and have bought interesting vessels, boxes, etc to hold home-made things, so, next month and in December I'm going to start producing homemade sweets and cakes to package up as Xmas presents.

This month feels like a bit of a disaster because I'm certainly not putting in the time like I have been every other month – but maybe that isn't the point. On a completely different note, last month's competition month has again paid off with ... another bug book. We must have both entered these competitions – and maybe virtually no one else did. However, they will make good Xmas presents for a couple of the kids we know.

Saturday 31st October

Well, it's the end of the month and very little has been accomplished over the last week. I'm no further ahead on Xmas presents, but in a way I couldn't really be as I've now decided what I'm doing for everyone and the only thing I need now is time. Daisy and I are still to make another couple of presents (ceramic ones) but I don't want her to get fed up with doing this so will space it out over the next few weeks. As for friends, they'll all be getting home made chocolates, biscuits and cakes packaged in lovely, interesting second-hand jars. I'm not really sure what the shelf life is on these foodstuffs yet, so I've done ... nothing.

So, challenge over – was it fun or very challenging – no – I think I can safely say this was a bit of a dud. On to greater things...

Chapter 11 – November

Gaining a Skill

This is a real toughie for me. The idea is to see how much knowledge or skill can be achieved at something within a month. For Matt, this will fit in very well with his trying-to-be-self employed life at the moment because he is going to try to set up his own website from scratch. At the moment he knows absolutely nothing about the subject so he's keen to make a start. I know it'll conflict with some of my ideas because if he's fiddling about with the computer when I think he should be searching for work I already know how I can be ... and pregnant as well – multiply this by ten – poor old Matt.

For myself I'm finding it hard to think of a skill I'm capable of learning or doing in my condition (i.e. with a serious lack of concentration, without doing anything physical, not costing too much money and something which makes allowances for me being unable to sit still too long). I've toyed with several different ideas – learn a language, learn to sew (which I can't do at all but as I have no sewing machine I'm not sure how well I'd do), learn about Facebooky-type things (social networking, is it called?), plan a wedding and honeymoon (which I just may be too emotional to do at the moment) or the one I've ultimately decided on which is ... cake making (I know it sounds too boring to be true, but I can honestly say that although I'm a fairly good and experimental cook I am an absolutely terrible baker and cake maker. Every cake I've ever made has been pretty horrible, barely rising above the top of the sandwich tin and usually glued together to resemble a couple of slices of toast with jam in the middle.

I'm not too excited about this challenge from the offset as I can imaging we'll be eating a lot of horrible cakes but you never know – I was extremely excited about last month's challenge and ended up not enjoying it at all, so you never can tell. I've spoken to friends who actually bake and they tell me that apparently my slapdash behaviour (i.e. chucking in more or less ingredients as I see fit) just won't do and that I must become much more disciplined than usual. I'm hoping that I can improve to such an extent that I'll be able to use some of my offerings for Xmas presents. I'm going to keep my digital camera to hand so you should be able to judge for yourself how I'm doing.

Sunday 1st November

It's 10 o'clock at night and I've just had my second slice of the most risen cake I've ever made. It certainly wasn't perfect – it was a bit crunchy on the top and bottom. I thought that was because I may have left it in the oven a tad too long but Matt (who did Home Economics in school, as he keeps telling me) said it was because I had too much sugar in it. Anyway, for the first time ever I tried to follow the recipe for a Victoria sandwich to the letter but soon realised I had to juggle a bit. I was meant to put greaseproof paper in the tin – but didn't have any so buttered it instead. Unfortunately they stuck and didn't exactly come out looking even. I also realised I only had large instead of medium eggs so very roughly guessed quantities and chucked some of the fourth egg away. Lastly, I had run out of icing sugar for the butter icing and for on top of the cake so I tried to make some in my grinder-thingy which I had never used before (by whizzing up caster

138

sugar). Again, not exactly perfect. So, although tasty (filled with butter icing and lemon curd), and at least two day's worth of eating, I haven't really stuck to the advice to follow this as an exact science. Still, it was more light and airy than ever before (after whisking lots of air into it and gently folding in flour – how Delia) so I'm quite pleased with the result for day one.

Tuesday 3rd November

A couple of days have passed since I made my first cake of the month and I've had time to reflect on it. Now anyone who has been paying attention in the book will realise that food is important to Matt and I. The very fact that yesterday we had a sliver of cake each and today I threw the remaining half of the cake in the bin should be some indication of exactly how yummy it was! I was going to bake again today but instead have spent time reading recipes for different cakes and sweets for Xmas presents. I think I'd better have a run through of any I am planning to make to see if they are actually edible. I'm about to start making a list of ingredients then I am going to do a supermarket run tomorrow morning.

Saturday 7th November

It's 9pm and I'm in bed feeling a bit sick as I've made a complete glutton of myself tonight. Over the last couple of days I've been making confectionary in a test run for making Xmas presents next month. I've never attempted anything like this before and although it is not strictly baking I am following recipes in a cake book and they're most definitely sweet – my feelings of nausea tonight can attest to that!

The reason I've been making them over two days is that they need time to harden. I've now made peppermint creams (half covered and wholly covered in chocolate) and roasted hazelnut and raisin clusters covered in Belgian chocolate. I couldn't eat the peppermint creams, mainly because I don't like mint creams but also because they contain egg white which remains uncooked (which I'm not meant to touch during pregnancy). I'm now quite glad I can't eat them as I suspect the fifteen or so chocolate clusters I've devoured tonight have been enough.

It's strange but I'm now spending loads of time thinking about my challenges. On one hand I'm getting tired of having to think of new things to do all the time, but on the other I'm extremely competitive (with myself) and desperately want to end the year of challenges with a good or meaningful challenge. At the start of the year I had so many ideas but as time has gone on I've either changed my priorities or my pregnancy or Matt's redundancy has changed our abilities to take part in certain activities due to lack of stamina, health or monetary restrictions.

We did manage to solve one of our big financial challenges this morning. I happened to run into one of the parents of a girl I used to teach a couple of weeks ago. I noticed that she had a big muckle car of the type we were looking for. When I spoke to her about it she said she was looking for a smaller car as this was a second car to her family, so this morning we swapped my car and a few hundred quid for her 7 seater people carrier. I was sorry to see my gold (topaz or 'bling a bling bling' car go, as Daisy called it) but it's a huge relief to have been able to get the size of car we need without much money having to change hands. I've also had another offer of a double buggy with integral bassinettes (!? – not too sure what they are either) from another parent of twins I teach, so we will shortly be going to collect that in our sturdy, big car. We have been so lucky so far – lots of mates and acquaintances have really come through for us and have offered us almost everything we will need for the twins. The offers couldn't have come at a better time and we are eternally grateful. I think next month's challenge may be based on how lucky we feel in so many ways just now. Having said that, my gratitude can be hard to distinguish when I'm over-emotional and moaning at Matt about the mess in the house (as I've just done again within the last hour), am grumping at Daisy for demanding her own way (we thought the terrible twos were over – seems like they may have just been delayed a lot with our lovely child) or when I'm complaining to anyone who will listen about my sore back, indigestion or worse (don't want to put anyone off their dinner). I am very aware we must remember (in the midst of pregnancy and unemployment worries) how incredibly fortunate we are compared to many, many others.

Friday 13th November
Well I have continued to try making confectionary but with, I'm afraid, pretty disastrous results. Two nights ago I spent AGES making tablet, having heard that the P6's in our school had successfully made tablet that day. I couldn't believe how much stirring it took and even worse, I've never really thought about what was in tablet before. In case you don't know – sugar, sugar, sugar, sugar, condensed milk and butter – how incredibly healthy! Well, I waited on it setting – and waited – and waited. It's now had two nights in the fridge and still isn't exactly set looking, so I guess I've not really made this according to plan. I was meant to

142

use a shallow tin and didn't – my plan of following instructions exactly didn't last too long. I'm also finding the tablet too sweet to eat (pregnancy? – this has never been a problem before) so I've also made a batch of Mars bar and raisin slices for weekend treats. I can hardly claim this as a new skill though as Mars bar slice is a regular favourite of ours. I added the raisins after again trying the incredibly sweet tablet and thinking more fruit was needed in our diet...

Monday 16th November

The challenge for the month is, at the moment, at a complete standstill. By the time you read this my diary may not make any sense as I'm sure time will distort what I'm about to say, but ... PANIC has occurred here over the weekend. I am 26 weeks pregnant and I've got swine flu. This 'epidemic' is extremely scary at the moment as a pregnant woman has recently died of it in my local hospital. Indeed pregnant women are one of the most vulnerable groups and have been advised to take the vaccine against getting this flu. My health visitor had called a couple of weeks ago to say the vaccine was in at the health centre but I had not taken it. I had given it lots and lots of thought but Thalidomide kept coming to mind (which was offered to my mum when she was pregnant with me and which she always used as a cautionary tale against taking any unnecessary medicines). As the swine flu vaccine has not had much research yet I decided against it. I think it's just been incredibly bad luck that I have now come down with it.

I went to the hospital on Saturday afternoon with trouble breathing and was diagnosed with a chest infection (which I expected). Whilst there I was routinely swabbed for swine flu as I displayed one of the many symptoms (a cough). Yesterday I got a call saying the test had come back positive and I had to come straight to the hospital where I was kept in isolation while several masked people came backwards and forwards. I ended up having an x-ray (much to my consternation) to determine that I did not have pneumonia and was sent away with an anti-viral drug called Relenza. Being the way I am, I refused to take this either, until I had come home and done as much research as possible on the internet. Having said that, after much reading, I feel none the wiser but I have accepted medical advice and have taken the drug. Not happy about it though.

The thought as well as the practicalities of November's challenge are now out of the window. Not only am I unable to go over the door for a week but (having just chucked my fairly unsuccessful tablet in the bin when it turned all runny and squidgy) there is no way I want to prepare food for anyone when I am full of germs.

I'm going to spend a wee bit of time thinking tonight about the challenges. I hate the thought of things tailoring off towards the end of the year – I really wanted to go out with a bang, but, at the moment and with this challenge that just doesn't seem at all possible. I am going to be having the next couple of weeks off work and although we're not putting Daisy into nursery (so no-one else panics) I think I'll be going stir crazy stuck in the house and would maybe benefit from having another challenge to get my teeth into. Should I use this time productively or should I just put my very tired feet up and try to relax? – I'll tell you tomorrow.

Saturday 21st November

I would think this'll be the last entry I'll make in my diary for November, for two reasons.

Firstly I think my laptop is about to break down again (Matt managed to fix it at the start of the year but the problem is recurring) and we don't have the money to renew if it's unfixable.

Secondly, I am absolutely cheesed off at the moment. The strain is finally getting to both Matt and I and we have been finding it increasingly difficult to get on. I think the main strain has been from his redundancy. He's now been unemployed for almost 4 months and I think he's started to get really disheartened about the job situation. I sometimes feel that he's not trying as hard as I want him to try to find work, but, in reality he's between a rock and a hard place. I don't want him to take a job anymore because I want him here for when the twins are born and until I get over my caesarean section operation. So, he's been desperately trying to claw in some work self employed but it's just not happening. He has registered with virtually every employment agency in Edinburgh and has posted off hundreds of applications or letters of interest. So, our reality just now is that Matt tries to bring in work (though doesn't like trying to make phone calls when Daisy and I are in the house (where the bloody hell we're meant to go god only knows) and I'm desperately trying to save money with everything I'm doing and fretting about how we can make this situation last for another 4 or 5 months. I'm also worrying that he will end up taking a minimum pay job with hours which mean we can't be together for the rest of this pregnancy or when the twins are born, as at the moment we need money to go towards household expenses, never mind the hundreds of pounds it has cost to buy the basic insurances and equipment to enable him to try his hand at self-employed life (a fraction of which has been brought in).

Next ... my swine flu ... my breathing has started to improve but I am absolutely wiped out and have no reserves for anything or anyone in my life barring meeting Daisy's immediate needs. I'm just about to finish the concoction of medications I have been given but they have not only upset my immune system but I am walking about feeling permanently sick and exhausted.

Lastly, my pregnancy – I am now 27 weeks pregnant and feel like the size of a bus. I took the car to Sainsbury's this morning to do a shop as we had run out of everything and I got blocked in so I couldn't open the car door wide enough for myself. Guess who had done it? A nun! I asked her if she could move her car as I couldn't get into mine and she retorted (not with the best humour) that perhaps I should park over two spaces next time. What did I do? Got in the car and cried. I'm sure she didn't mean it unkindly but I'm well and truly at the end of my tether just now. So forgive me for my sudden absence but I can't face any more challenges in life at the moment – I can barely face getting up in the morning.

Chapter 12 – December

Peace, Goodwill and Relaxation to All Men

Especially me!

This one's a no brainer really and re-reading the previous page I can see it was a long time coming. Matt and I had spent many a night thinking about how we could finish the year on a positive note and whereby we'd be thinking about others rather than ourselves, but, with the way things have been for us lately we both feel it'd be just too hard to be completely selfless at the moment.

Ideas we had knocked around over the year for the last challenge of the year were to do charitable work for a month (we decided we didn't want to start and then withdraw from something though as it wouldn't be fair to others), to become as environmentally friendly as possible (we knocked that one on the head when we realised Daisy wasn't yet ready to give up her night-time nappies and we had no intention of going to washable at this stage of the game – also, can you imagine how difficult it would be to have an environmentally friendly Xmas - a challenge to be sure but one which I intend to look at again next year) or to become much more pro-active when it comes to politics and the things which dictate how we live our lives and shape our environment. However, when faced with this final month and the way we feel we've decided we need to change our lives on a much smaller and more manageable scale.

Tuesday 1st December

We've started small – we invited our friends Morag, Ben and Sol for dinner even although Morag keeps insisting that they should be looking after me in my advanced pregnant state. To be honest, I love entertaining and they're such relaxing company that it isn't a hardship at all. A lovely night was had by all and Ben even approached me to potentially do some work for his company (helping to write academic material to be used on educational software). Much as this month is meant to be about relaxation I think I'm going to take him up on it since the money has hardly been pouring into our household lately.

Thursday 3rd December

My second attempt at goodwill this month – I attended a meeting for my local authority education department to try to help or encourage other teachers to think about going for chartered status, as I have. I do think this is incredibly worthwhile, but if I hadn't arranged to go to this in advance or wasn't trying to think about others, I doubt I'd have went along, as it constituted a 14 hour day from leaving home in the morning to getting back at night. I was absolutely done in and my ankles were the size of balloons but I'm glad I went.

Monday 7th December

I have spent the whole weekend making gifts for others either as Xmas presents or as token gifts to let people know we're thinking about them. I made about 500 sweeties (peppermint creams, either green, white or covered in chocolate – all cut out as little hearts, stars or snowflakes) and they're delicious. I've spent ages tonight dividing them up into little bags (15 in total) and am going to spend tomorrow wrapping them beautifully with ribbon, etc. Matt's not entirely sure how the homemade presents will go down with everyone he knows but I'm pretty sure that most of my mates will truly be pleased to have had some thought put into their gifts (I hope so at least).

The peace part of the challenge hasn't really happened so far this month. You wouldn't believe the pain-in-the-arse situations we've had so far this month as far as domesticity goes. I won't bore you with the details but after a weekend of seeing boiler maintenance people, roofing contractors and heating engineers, Matt had today cut a big bloody hole in out bathroom ceiling to try to find out where or how water is getting into our house. Aaaaaargh! Surprisingly I'm taking this all a bit better than expected and am trying to stay laid back about the whole thing. Even my impending work on the education project (which I should really start now) isn't getting me too bothered (although I'm sure it crept into my dreams last night). Just the very act of typing this is probably doing me some good at focussing me on what should be happening this month, i.e. relaxation and peace – so with that in mind I'm off to make my lovely and grubby man a cup of coffee and then I'm going to lie down amid the mess and put my feet up for a couple of hours.

Wednesday 9th December

Today has been one of the most relaxing days I can remember in ages. We're back in Edinburgh and this morning Matt took Daisy out to give me a break. I wandered along to the Metropole, my favourite cafe, and savoured a bacon roll whilst reading BOTH the Scotsman and the Times. Bliss! I then waddled along (feeling like the babies have dropped so I'm walking in a rather strange manner) to the video shop and hired the film 'Coco before Chanel' which I've just watched. I watched most of it on the computer as, being subtitled, I've discovered that my rapidly deteriorating eyes (along with the rest of me) just don't function the way they used to. It was a lovely film, made all the better with the arrival of a surprise package for me. I'VE WON ANOTHER PRIZE - this time one I actually really want – a boxed set of 6 Audrey Hepburn DVDs. This is definitely being kept as a treat for alongside my Hotel Chocolat chocolates (which I'm sure Matt will get me for Xmas considering the amount of very heavy hints I've made).

So, peace – tick, goodwill – tick (I was extremely nice to Matt today) and relaxation – tick. A good day, all in all.

Monday 14th December

Ho ho ho – I feel like a jolly, fat Santa. Jolly, because the hole in the roof is still not worrying me unduly, even though we have not found the reason for it. Fat, because ... well at least I have a good excuse and Santa because I feel like a bringer of goodwill and very yummy peppermint creams to people who are being nice to us or who we think deserve a treat. We even (royal 'we' – Matt, I mean) even made up a new batch at the weekend after our friends Myra and John had been for dinner and had been raving about the look of our gift packages. We gave them their own little package this morning. This afternoon I'm going to take our paediatric consultant one for a gift as I think, or hope, he may be doing us a very big favour soon.

On another wee note, my excitement over winning the Audrey Hepburn prize was short-lived. My dad had apparently renewed a subscription to Hello magazine for me for Xmas (my guilty secret pleasure) and the

DVD set had come with it as a complimentary gift. So far, not too impressed with our competition success!

Peace, goodwill and relaxation – I think we're just about managing it. Matt and I haven't fought in ages so the stress is obviously subsiding (for me at least). I think I must be getting accustomed to the fact that he isn't working and at the moment I certainly don't want him taking another job. I have, however, been working fairly non-stop at my second job, writing educational material. I agreed as I think this may lead to more work in the future (which we will no doubt desperately need) but it's also good for my own professional development. Now, as a fairly obsessive person this task is now on my mind constantly, even though I am only about half way through it, but in a week's time I aim to be finished, a bit richer, feeling a bit more accomplished and sitting with my feet up reading a Hello magazine and awaiting Santa Claus. Matt thinks I'm mad taking this on. He knows how tired I am at the moment and because this is the first time I've done this kind of work it will take me a lot of research, time and energy for the amount of money involved. My reasoning is, however, I will get quicker and quicker so next time … Plus I hate to turn down a challenge (Quelle surprise – non?).

Tuesday 22nd December
It's Tuesday afternoon, 3.15pm and I'm typing this from bed. I'm not ill, just shattered and my darling Matty is giving me a chance for a rest. The snow has been falling and now the pavements are slippery and although I had made plans to go out this afternoon I've instead decided to take the more sensible or selfish route and curl up in my bed to catch up on this diary.

I've finished my job for our friend Ben. I worked fairly constantly at it during the weekend and I'm glad to report he was pleased with my efforts. He's asked if I would look at other areas in education for him and although I'm seriously tempted to just start right away, I'm, for one, going to be sensible and have said I'm not going to think about it at all until after the Xmas break.

I've also now given out most of the Xmas peppermint sweeties we made. Some were given in the form of Secret Santa presents – I'm not sure how that went down to be honest – some of the recipients I'm sure would have appreciated a thoughtful home-made gift, but others ... not too sure. We've also given out lots of bags so people we just wanted to say thank you to, for example, great pals, our consultant at the hospital (who is taking a great deal of interest in the challenges every time I see him for an ante natal appointment (most encouraging), Daisy's child care places and to a couple of the lovely mums who have helped me in the school – one who helps every week in the classroom (a complete godsend and now a good pal) and to another who has loaned us a fantastic double buggy, saving us a fortune in the process. So, all in all, the handmade presents (most of which certainly seem to have been appreciated) have gone a great way to our goodwill part of the challenge.

As for the relaxation part – well I'm hoping that can truly start now that I've finished my job. The only thing which could interrupt that is going into labour early and as I type I keep having what I hope are Braxton Hicks contractions so I hope it's not imminent.

The peace part of the challenge – harder. As any of you know who have a three and a half year old at home (I'm hoping this doesn't just relate to my little angel anyway), December is not lending itself easily to a time for quiet reflection. Daisy is completely wild at the moment. The fact that she spent the morning with Matt at Winter Wonderland in Edinburgh (after having already been with the nursery this week) means Santa is never far from her thoughts and although she wakes up every morning and says things like "I'll never be naughty again" she just can't help herself. Her phraseology is by the way, self inflicted – I'm realistic enough to know that no 3 year old should promise to be good for longer than an hour or two, max.

Tomorrow is my birthday and Matt has said he'll let me start the day with a big lie in bed. We're also going out to lunch – nothing too fancy (my choice) as I feel spending too much money at the moment would be a bit of a waste, but it's at a bistro outside the centre of town so I should be able to park the car and waddle the few steps to the restaurant and back without too much trouble.

I'm off now to check my e-mails then either snuggle down with my hot water bottle to continue reading the Ben Elton novel I've just started or to watch an Audrey Hepburn movie from my new DVD collection. Life ain't bad.

Thursday 31ˢᵗ December – the final day
It feels fairly surreal to be making what is effectively the last diary entry in this journal. I'm still at home, still very, very pregnant and still trying to make sure that the holidays are spent in a relaxing manner. We are having the strangest Xmas and New Year I have ever experienced. We got stuck in Edinburgh on the run up to Xmas. Unfortunately all Daisy's presents and our Xmas dinner were stuck in the Borders at the same time. On Christmas Eve, therefore, panic set in a bit to Matt and I and we scooted out to the shops to buy

something for Daisy just in case Santa didn't realise where we'd be in the morning. Luckily he obliged and Daisy not only got a lovely jewellery box delivered to the Edinburgh flat but it also came with a note from Santa explaining that he had in fact delivered all her presents as previously requested to the Borders. Anyway, long story short, we managed to drive down to the Borders on Xmas afternoon and all was saved and the turkey dinner was had by almost all – Matt, Daisy, my dad and I, although unfortunately my auntie and cousin who had planned to spend the day with us didn't want to push their luck and make the drive in case they got stuck. Strangely enough, even with all the uncertainty of the situation I took things remarkably calmly and hardly fretted at all. I'm not sure if the challenge had anything to do with it but for the moment I feel I've got much bigger things to think about in the near future.

The week since Xmas has been lovely down here at the cottage. Not only has it snowed almost every day making it almost impossible for us to go out (I'm trying not to think of the potential of being stuck, unable to get to a hospital, if I go into labour) but Daisy has been so happy with her toys (a lot of which had the ability to keep her amused by herself for a while), that she has been an absolute delight to be around. We've spent the week face and hand painting, playing 'Build a Beetle', lacing card pictures, playing with fuzzy felt or have been on the CBeebies website on the computer. Matt now has a chest infection and is fairly poorly, but even so (how unsympathetic do I sound – I do feel sympathetic but at least it's when he can relax and take it easy) we're both managing to spend much of our days relaxing – we're simply taking it in turns to watch Daisy or to lounge about in front of the blazing coal fire

– worse ways to spend the festivities I'd say. Also, as for tonight, for the first New Year's Eve in many years, I don't actually care what we or anyone else is doing. Normally I spend ages thinking about what we should do at the bells and hate to hear about other people's invitations to great parties if we have few plans, but this year although we've been asked out to a few places (and some we'd have really liked to have taken up) we've instead chosen to buy a couple of huge big fillet steaks, a tiny little bottle of red wine and are planning to light the fire, get Daisy to bed and have a lovely romantic dinner together while we still can. It brings back so many memories of when Daisy was born. I clearly remember making a big steak dinner one night a couple of months after she was born and recall our frustration of eventually having to eat our tepid meals individually whilst the other tried desperately to rock her to sleep. To think we've got that all coming up again soon, but in tandem. God, it's scary but at the same time I can't wait to meet them. They're kicking hard just now and lying so low I get the feeling I'm not going to have to wait too long.

Our preparation for the twins has certainly helped me relax quite a bit this month. We've spent a fortune on plastic boxes and are now all sorted out as far as clothes, bedding etc goes. Matt has been a star because although I had started to sort out all the clothes and had managed to sort most out for Edinburgh and some for the Borders, we have since been given loads more and this task has fallen exclusively to Matt – partly because I can't bend and pick up comfortably anymore and partly because I am now losing interest. Having said that my nest building is kicking in a bit again and I'm seriously thinking about gutting the cottage to get rid of much of the junk built up over the previous 22 years.

So, was this challenge a success? Peace, goodwill and relaxation to all? I think considering the year we've had, with 8 months of the pregnancy being somewhat overshadowed by 5 months of Matt's unemployment (and, I've got to say the biggest strain I have personally ever experienced in my life, never mind poor old Matt who has coped with his situation and with my bloody moods rather admirably), this year has ended remarkably peaceably, particularly between Matt and I. We're coming to the end of the year still in love, still happy with each other and still, despite the bickering, huffing and puffing which has gone on this year, looking forward to taking the next step of our lives together.

Goodwill? We've done our best and tried to think of others throughout the month, whether this was in the form of home-made gifts, thoughtful phone calls or invitations to dinner etc. Whether this has been noticed at all we've no idea and it doesn't matter anyway – our intention was simply to try.

Relaxation? I could be glib and say, try hauling about a couple of bowling balls in your uterus and see how relaxed you feel, but in actual fact, despite my fairly consistent moaning to Matt about the trivial effects of pregnancy (lack of sleep, indigestion, discomfort, aching back, etc) I'm feeling pretty relaxed at the moment. I also feel that what's about to happen is out-with my control to a huge extent so this may be contributing to my state of mind. Matt and I have also spoke at length about his employment situation and have decided that although he can't realistically look for work just now, the self employed situation hasn't taken off this year, so after the twins are born he's going to get stuck in to searching for any type of work that's available whilst still keeping the option of the business going (without spending any more in the process). Not an ideal situation, but we are a lot luckier than some. I still have a job I can go back to if need be, Matt could be a househusband (a role he's willing and quite happy to do) or we could try to think up a wee business between us which could hopefully bring in a few bucks. So, as I say, luckier than some and in the other ways which matter to us - much, much, much luckier than most we know.

Have the challenges of the past year had any lasting effects on our lives? What do you think? I'd be kidding you if I said we'd been affected by them all, but some have touched our lives so strongly that I wouldn't go back to before them for anything (slight exaggeration there – wads of dosh could persuade me to do almost anything at the moment). I now intend to spend the start of 2010 telling you exactly what effect our little experiment had on us. Whether this is a condensed passage or two or a lengthy exploration of our lives to date is dependent on two things – both of which Daisy keeps telling me she hears saying, "gag a goo goo, let us out, Merry Xmas". We'll see ....!

Chapter 13

Update

I can't quite believe so much time has passed since I last put pen to paper or fingers to a keyboard, but ... it's now March 31st 2010 and the ONLY reason I know that is because it's my 'big girl's' birthday tomorrow. I can now say my 'big girl' for I also have a 'little girl' and a 'little boy'. Kitty and Oliver were born on the 22nd of January after a day filled with 'fun and excitement'. I started having contractions at lunchtime the previous day while I was having lunch with my auntie and cousin in Edinburgh. They stopped and started and were extremely infrequent so I decided (stupidly I was told by my lunch companions and everyone since) to drive back to the Borders so I could go to the same hospital in which I had Daisy. Realising this was indeed fairly silly I asked my dad to meet me half way in case I had to 'jump' cars. However, all felt well and we made it to the hospital without any problems. They duly told me the head was only three fifths engaged and I wouldn't be having these babies anytime soon and so I was sent home. I went home and got into my bed about eleven at night only to be awoken with a bang two hours later when my waters broke fairly explosively. Trying not to panic I called my friends to watch Daisy. One by one (3 different households) they ignored the phone (being at one in the morning they couldn't hear it and as I was over 4 weeks early none of them were prepared) so by the time a further 20 minutes had passed I went into a state of mild panic. I called my dad who said he'd make the 30 minute journey as quickly as possible and then I also managed to get our friend Sean to come and watch Daisy till my dad arrived. Sean got here very, very quickly to find me with a towel wrapped round my waist, furry fake- Ugg boots on (the only footwear I could fit into) and amniotic fluid running down my legs. Lovely! We then called an ambulance and by the time it reached the house (10 or 15 minutes later) my contractions were becoming regular. Indeed by the time I got to the hospital 40 minutes later at two thirty in the morning they were 3 minutes apart. I then entered 'Casualty' mode – a 'team were assembled' (hospital speak) – rather a large team it turned out, as we were having premature twins, and at 4.29 and 4.31am respectively, 6lb 9 oz Kitty, then breech, 7lb 6oz Oliver, were born by Caesarean section.

Our lovely big babies came back to my room with me for the day but by evening I still hadn't managed to produce enough milk for them so they were taken to the SCBU (Special Care Baby Unit). They stayed there for 3 days and we stayed in hospital for a week in total and as soon as I could persuade them that I could breast feed these two hungry babies by myself I got home. Neither of us could believe at first how easy it was looking after them – they slept most of the day and night and were easily satisfied with the amount of milk I was producing. Oh how times have changed! They are now 9 weeks old and are doing well but no longer have the sleepiness of premature babies and we are surviving on an average of 3 or 4 hours of broken sleep a night. Last night we got 7 hours broken into 5 and 2 hour portions and consequently I now feel rested enough to have an attempt at updating this for the first time in 3 months. Feeding is a whole other different story. I am determined to exclusively breast feed which meant that one day last week I was sitting on the couch for 8 hours solid with trips only to the kitchen and bathroom. Oliver is a sicky wee baby who most of the time regurgitates rather a lot of his milk – hence at times my life is a round of feeding Oliver, winding Oliver, watching him being sick, feeding Kitty, winding Kitty, putting Kitty down to sleep and then returning to Ollie. Luckily the 8 hour stint is the exception rather than the rule and most days I am managing to scrabble together something resembling a real life. We have in fact managed a rather good weekend whereby I went out with the girls from the village on Friday for a meal and to a folk music night and Matt and I got out with the twins the following evening to a fancy dress party (with the twins – sssssshhh, don't tell Daisy, it was a no-kids except breast-fed kids allowed). We had an absolute ball and although we only stayed an hour and three quarters (as we had to get Daisy up for a night-time pee and didn't want to have to ask her granddad to do it) it felt like we were getting our life back. So much so that I really didn't want to come home and was quite unashamedly stroppy about it.

Daisy is being a wonderfully caring big sister and is helping choose clothes and change the twins' nappies, but understandably she is finding the sudden disruption to our household difficult at times. Knowing how to wind me up (as all kids do), last week, after a marathon 3 hour session with me of cutting, gluing, making photo albums and playing princess stuff she queried, "why don't you pay me any attention anymore?" I quietly snivelled to Matt about how sad this made me. He, being a bloke and not remotely as emotional as me said, "she's winding you up" and happily ignored her later outbursts of, "I've had enough of the twins", "I've had enough of this house" and later in the day when looking at playhouses in a local playhouse sales centre (when being told off and threatened with non acquisition of playhouse for being naughty), "I don't need a new playhouse, I've already got one in my bedroom" (a plastic cheapy one in the Borders) was told swiftly by Matt that that one could be chopped up and thrown in the bucket pronto. As Matt says, "she's winding me up" ... but ... it must be really hard for her to see us both at times with babes in our arms and, well, I'm a big sucker. On that point, the 'big' part, one really good consequence of being run off my feet is that not only am I consuming more food than ever before, including an enormous amount of yummy yummy goodies, BUT I am now 9lb lighter than before I got pregnant. I truly recommend to all you women, who like me, were constantly thinking about your weight – go and have twins – or triplets – or quads – a breeze. I've clearly lost my marbles!

Back to the present. Tomorrow is Daisy's 4th birthday. We're going to a big new soft play in Edinburgh with her best friend, Solomon, and on Saturday she's having her much asked for 'princess party' where she is having not one, but two friends to play (Wow – we're really pushing the boat out!). I would tell you more of these exciting plans just now but two little beings have just started screaming at the top of their lungs. Over and out!

Chapter 14

Revisiting the Year

If you're reading this then I'm assuming this book has been published though at the moment (on 12th April 2010) I cannot imagine how this came to pass. I've had the first chance in a couple of weeks to sit for a few moments at the computer again as the twins are, for once, asleep. Occasionally we seem to have broken past the pain barrier and actually manage a fairly good night's sleep, then before we can actually say, "thank you" in case a higher power is listening, randomness seems to kick in again and the next night generally consists of 3 hours broken catnaps. Last night was pretty good – I think we had about 5 hour's straight sleep and today we were not only able to hold some semblance of a conversation at dinner but I'm also managing to type this. However, on a normal day-to-day basis I have no idea how I'm ever going to continue writing let alone think about trying to get it published.

Although I have not yet had the chance to formally review my year I have a feeling I may have failed at as many tasks as succeeded. This is not to say my year has been without success and I can categorically say I have learned more about myself, my relationship with Matt, my values, my positive attributes and my shortcomings than in any other period in my life. I truly believe the experiment we embarked upon has given us a real opportunity for growth as individuals and as a family and apart from all that it's been FUN to test our abilities and push our boundaries from our normal behaviours.

I intend now to revisit every challenge, re-read my own notes and make an up to date commentary as to whether at the one year on stage we have made any significant changes in the way we live our lives. Do I have any pearls of wisdom for you, dear reader? – Read on and see!

Chapter 15 – Revisiting January

Needs and Not Wants

This is so weird. I am writing this book so disjointedly. It is now May 2010 and I am only just getting another chance to look at my challenges again. I've just reread my entries from January and it's been lovely to revisit our lives and be reminded of what we were experiencing as a family of three. It also brings to the fore the kind of year we've had. If ever there was a year when we needed to know how we would survive in times of stress and economic difficulties then this was it.

Little did we know at the start of the year that instead of thinking about holiday plans we would have to think of how to survive a very, very long period of redundancy. Matt has now been out of work for ten months and at last we are seeing a light at the end of the tunnel. He starts his new job in two weeks which is just as well as I will now only be receiving statutory maternity pay.

So, how have our lives changed? Well, there's an interesting dichotomy now present in our lives. We now consciously live much more economically. We eat out a lot less often and when we do we consider it a treat, not just a routine occurrence. We very rarely order takeaways, having decided that the food I cook is almost invariably better and with forward planning can be just as quick. We also order our food online saving money on impulse buys. I could pretend this is just about saving money but with 3 children under 5 in tow I doubt this is an outing I really want to make.

Daisy still gets lots of 'treats' but for the past few months she has bought most of them herself from the huge bank of change in her piggy banks. Counting out hundreds of coppers and piles of silver money, I hope makes her begin to understand the value of money.

Matt seems to have really benefitted from this challenge. When we first met he kept a record of his spending on a spreadsheet and gave himself a monthly allowance for 'fun'. I argued with him that 'woo hoo' lots of fun was unlikely on £20 a month (he keeps saying it was a week but I think he just doesn't want to seem too much of a saddo). Although I thought he was a bit 'tight' shall I say, his ethos and the reminder set by this challenge has served him well this year and he's hardly touched a penny save from the absolute necessities.

HOWEVER, and this is a huge however from both of us – the main thing that this challenge has changed, is making us evaluate our spending and prioritise our needs and wishes in order to achieve the best quality of life. Three weeks ago, when we were completely consumed by lack of sleep, lack of individual time away from children and completely at cracking level with each other, we came to a decision. We needed to find a way to each improve our lives in order to be able to survive with each other peaceably.

For the last few weeks I had been trying to persuade Matt that with his new job imminent we should be considering taking the children abroad this summer as this may be the best time to be able to travel with the twins. My reasoning was that they will still be immobile and can spend lots of time in the buggy while we can relax and don't have to run after them, Daisy is able to play easily by herself or makes friends quickly with other children, the twins' airfare is still free if they sit on our laps and lastly, we need a break. Matt wasn't keen. Although we've had some great holidays with Daisy when she was wee I think he has a better recollection of just how much 'stuff' we had to take abroad with one baby, let alone two and our 'big girl' as she wants called.

An alternative arrangement has been found. Wait for it... for less money, much less money than the trip abroad, I have joined one of the swankiest spas in Edinburgh where I plan to go three times a week (I've already managed this successfully for two weeks). It's gorgeous. It has an outdoor hydro pool, Cleopatra baths, a thermal suite and a great pool. I didn't pay the extra to join the gym part – this is after all meant to be, for me, all about relaxation. I had looked at spas which were cheaper but they either allowed children use the facilities at any time (and I'm trying to get away from mine!) or there was no Jacuzzi or a tiny pool. Now I know I'm sounding like a bit of a princess but hear me out.

Matt's wish list was cheaper to accommodate. His ultimate desire (really!) is to have 2 hours to himself 3 times a week to play computer games (and bless him, the ones he has bought were 3 for a tenner or twenty quid – he doesn't have expensive taste, except for his girlfriend that is) and his ultimate ambition is to build a super duper refrigerated computer. "What!!!!" I hear you ask. I'm just impressed that I was listening for long enough to be able to convey that information to you. All I do know is that for geeky Matt, Custom PC and all other things techy are his Holy Grail. He did, after all, on our first Christmas together, ask for rubber tubing. Kinky – non? Non – he wanted to put it inside his computer and run anti-freeze through it as a cooling system. Gosh, even as a type this I'm impressed with my knowledge – something must be going in after all with the hours of excited conversation he is sometimes intent on having!

So, that's me and Matt taken care of, but what about our poor wee bairns I hear you ask. Well they each get the benefit of having a relaxed and happy mummy and daddy but they're also going to get their holiday – or holidays I should say. We're buying a roof-boxy thing for our car, a 5 man tent and we're off on summer adventures this year. Morag, Ben and Sol are keen to come camping with us again and Daisy's already talking about fishing and barbeques at the campsite. Oliver and Kitty haven't protested yet – or even sat up yet for that matter – and assuming we get a typical British summer, they won't find themselves being overheated and sunburnt from the tropical climes.

All this AND we should still have money left over from what we would have spent on a foreign holiday. In conclusion to the January challenge – was it life changing – without a doubt. We now prioritise our spending, appreciate everything we've got and look forward to everything we carefully plan to treat ourselves to in the future. Do we take 'things' for granted? – Not on your life. We know Matt or I could be made redundant at any time, the financial market could continue to plunge deeper towards disaster or indeed any type of calamity could befall us, but, we know we'd try our best to work our way out of any situation and for that we're eternally grateful.

Chapter 16 - Revisiting February

Attention to detail

Let me first begin with Matt, as this challenge was, after all, predominantly chosen by him and for him. Little did we know in these cold February mornings that Matt would soon have to simply choose between working-in-the-garden jeans and less-like-working-in-the-garden jeans for the best part of the next year. He hung up his suit (save for interviews and job seeking) at the end of July and has barely considered his dress code again until this weekend. It's now mid May 2010 and Matt will be starting his new job, again as a Chartered Quantity Surveyor on Monday. As yet he doesn't exactly know the dress code in the office but I suspect he will very hastily enquire to me on Sunday night, "Which of these shirts is the whitest?", again taking us right back to where we started the challenge. So, there were few lasting changes in Matt's life. As for me, well things took a more surprising turn...

You may remember I had little inclination to either do or stick with the challenge. The results were, now looking back, quite surprising to me. I continued throughout the year, clearing any clothes which were beyond repair – amazing considering I continued to wear shirts chewed by a friend's horse more than ten years ago. I also realised that I should try to dress the way I wanted to appear to others and with that in mind I started to clear any clothes which I thought made me look too matronly (which I had initially bought as 'sensible and smart-ish teaching clothes'. Things in good condition went to the charity shop – the absolute dross went in the bucket (should have been rag bags, I later realised) and, wait for it, I didn't replace the items but instead left spare room in my drawers.

Later in the year, when I found out I was pregnant I dug out my old maternity clothes and was topped up with cast offs from friends. It wasn't until the final few weeks that I actually had to cave and buy a couple of really cheap maternity skirts online as I was just too big to get into anything else comfortably. Now I have given birth and am returning to a 'normal' (though very changed) shape I have continued with my clear out. All my maternity gear has been given away as have lots of my shapeless and much-too-big-for-me tops which I have always favoured. The fact that I could continue to wear many of my 'normal' clothes until I was 7 months pregnant with twins alerted me reflect on how flattering exactly my clothes were. Matt keeps telling me to wear more fitted clothes – he reckons loose clothing does me no favours and much as I suspect he may have been watching too much fashion advice on breakfast telly (just kidding) I suspect he has a very good point.

So, gone – all the maternity clothes. Gone – lots of the shapeless, baggy clothing. Gone – lots of the boring, old fashioned, matronly gear. What am I left with? – Not very much which is wearable actually. Despite this being over the last 4 months I'm proud to say I've only bought one top costing £4, a pair of jeans for my post pregnancy figure and a new swimsuit for the spa as my pregnancy swimsuit was stretched beyond decency. Are my drawers, wardrobes and cupboards empty? Well, definitely emptier. But as my figure reduces they will continue to be even more so – I am determined to get rid of clothes which are way too big for me and may even start to be able to wear the vast majority of my wardrobe I have barely or never worn (being one of these people who have many, many times bought clothes to diet into). I'm not dieting (indeed I feel incredibly ill if I so much as miss a few snacks) but a mixture of breast feeding twins and running around after 3 children will, I am sure, help me shed at least a few pounds.

It is therefore, with great shock, that I can tell you this challenge turned out, against all odds, to be a minor success, for me, at least. It's even helped me incorporate some of the principles of frugality I learned with the January challenge.

Chapter 17 - Revisiting March

10 000 steps a day

This is the challenge which seems to have had the greatest influence on people. Quite a few of my friends have asked me where I bought my pedometer and have gone on to purchase one too. They too are trying to do the 10 000 steps a day. The thing which absolutely everyone has in common is that they are all shocked at how much walking you have to do to achieve this. I'm amazed that this is the government recommendation for everyone to be considered to have an active lifestyle as the very act of walking these step takes up such a large proportion of most people's free time.

Have I kept up with this challenge? The simple answer is no. I continue to walk – a lot – more than most people I know. I'm now doing this while pushing a double buggy and trying very often to keep up with my active four year old, but as far as counting the steps go I have stopped doing this. This is in part through the loss of the habit – whilst I was pregnant and exhausted I stopped most exercise apart from gentle walks and partly as I moved on to other challenges which were also time consuming. However, I've just re-read the March challenge diary and I had forgotten just how impressive the results were. With this in mind I'm thinking about getting the pedometer out of the bedside cabinet drawer and once again trying to develop a regular habit of 10 000 steps.

Did I ever use the fitness DVD? What do you think? It's gathering dust on my DVD shelf along with similar examples on Pilates, yoga, callisthenics, aerobics, you name it. What about my sit ups and push ups every day? Well here I at least have a good excuse. Since being pregnant with the twins my stomach muscles have separated and I've been told I must not do anything resembling a sit up until my muscles have improved – indeed I now get on and off the bed holding my stomach muscles in tightly to stop them bulging out – lovely picture, huh?

What about Matt? He's still walking as much as he ever did. Although he's obviously not been walking to work he thinks nothing of walking good distances around town and although neither of us have stuck to this challenge religiously we're both aware that this is a lifestyle we'd like to maintain – if only we had the energy left over by our 4 month old twins at the moment!

Chapter 18 - Revisiting April

Submissive wife / dominant husband challenge

Oh my God! – I've just re-read my April diaries and immediately 'got my fingers out' and worked out 9 months from that time ... to ... when the twins were born. So, it seems like this set of challenges had quite a long lasting effect! In my mind I'm sincerely hoping they were conceived in the beautiful country house hotel rather than simply in one of Matt's dominant moods. Oh – if only he'd known – that'll teach him!

Looking back, I'm not sure how much I learned from this challenge. True, I am a complete control freak and can be a complete nag – but I already knew that. It does, however, do me good to occasionally be reminded of the fact of how hard I can be to live with. I should try to re-read this chapter every week or so as I'm sure it'd tone my moods down a tad.

Has either of us changed? Essentially – no! Matt still sits back and waits for me to organise almost everything. He would, I'm sure, admit that on many matters he leaves the decisions to me and I hope he also recognises that this also means he leaves most of the legwork to me, especially in household and childcare matters, e.g. Daisy's nursery schooling, meal planning, holiday planning, shopping for food, clothes, furniture and the day to day running of the home.

I can't really recall, but I don't think I've been surprised again with a night out since last April, although pregnancy and changed economic circumstance have meant meals out haven't been high on our agendas.

Am I glad I took part in this challenge? – you betcha
I am – look what I got out of it!

Chapter 19 - Revisiting May

Creating an outdoor space

Well – you saw the pictures – Did we succeed?

As you saw, the changes were not massive, but we managed to give the gardens a 'bit of a tidy'. We have, to some extent, managed to maintain these changes. The perennial plants we put in have been a revelation. I'm going to spend the vast majority of my money from now on perennials as I'm writing this in July and the garden is in parts blooming with lovely colours from the delphiniums and, er, other 'things'. Today the sun is shining and we've spent lots of the day in the garden. Two wee squawking babes stop us from getting much accomplished but we don't care – we know we can, over time, make this a space we can cultivate over many years. Any time we think of getting rid of the cottage and losing our garden I think of Matt talking gently to the babies in the hospital last April when they were born and promising Oliver his very own fort and Kitty a fairy princess castle. Brings a tear to my eye – or would do if I didn't think of the huge list of jobs it'd have to follow (I jest, it's a lovely memory and a great dream)!

Chapter 20 - Revisiting June

Money, Money, Money

As I wipe a tear from my eye after re-reading this month's diary, I can look back and say what a wonderful, wonderful (note the 2 wonderfuls) result we had from the pregnancy. True, economically, worse was to come, but although things seemed bleak then I am writing this having come out the end of the tunnel.

It's just over a year since we faced these challenges. This may have been the month of the most boring challenge ever, but it did produce some results. My ISA has just matured and almost without thinking I contacted the bank to ask what interest I would now get (0.8%) and quickly changed it over to a new account offering 2.35% instead (all with the same conditions). Easy peasy and just required asking. Likewise I'm now aware of how much I spend on almost everything and constantly check out the best prices when renewing or buying anything.

Boring topic and boring reading for sure but I'm glad I'm taking the time to review the diaries. I had forgotten about my health scare. It's reminded me I need to make an appointment for a smear test as I've been putting this off since finding out I was pregnant and I should have gone within the last couple of months. Again, as we have a few times been reminded lately through friends' ill health, we are reminded that all that really matters is that we are all well – trite but true.

Chapter 21 - Revisiting July

No Telly

I will not surprise you here by saying ALL HAS RETURNED TO 'NORMAL'. What else can I say? – A clean house is not everything.

Chapter 22 - Revisiting August

Trying and cooking new foods

Looking back, I think this was one of our most interesting challenges. Everyone I have spoken to admits to the same behaviours as ours – that after a while we all rely on the same few recipes over and over again. It was definitely challenging to think of a new recipe for every day but has inspired us to try different foods even in a small way. Now when I am ordering a takeaway I frequently try something new and I have started buying many more ingredients or even frozen foods from the Indian and Chinese supermarkets in Edinburgh.

Having three children has meant that we do still use frozen, takeaway and convenience food. Although I am surprised to say, if anything, it is less than we did before. I now bulk cook several dishes per month and at the moment we have a large stock of shepherd's pies, beef carbonade, spaghetti bolognaise and spicy beef and bean curries in the freezer and, I'm proud to say that although I did try to make a quiche with readymade pastry we were so disappointed with the taste difference that I have continued to make my own pastry ever since and it's well worth it.

Out twins are now nearly six months old and during that time we've been out for one meal. This was to a restaurant situated in a residential country house where there is no choice of food and where the owner serves the ten or so guests in their own private dining room. Although none of the food was what I would have chosen off a menu (beef carpaccio, halibut then mangoes and ice cream) it was fantastic to have some time together when indulging one of our favourite hobbies – eating (sleeping would beat it every time just now). Tonight we've had an offer from my cousin for her and my dad to baby sit for us next Tuesday (as the twins have this week started trying solids so don't completely rely on my boobs) and although we've vaguely thought about what food we would like it's much more important for us to have time together. One thing is for sure – when we do go out I'm much more likely than before to be adventurous in my ordering since probably won't remember just another carbonara or ham and mushroom pizza but I will always remember the sweetbreads, jambalaya and marmite (??!!) I tried and will certainly remember the first time I made popcorn (as will the plastic dishes which ended up in the bucket as a consequence.

Chapter 23 - Revisiting September

Competitions

– <u>all 658 of them</u>

I hope you, like many of my friends are waiting with bated breath for the response to this month's competition entering. Matt and I BOTH WON !
 ... the same competition
 ... the same prize
 ... wait for it
 ... the £4.99 Dorling Kindersley book about bugs which you already know about ...

Apart from that, NADA ! Having said that, ever the optimist, I keep entering more and more. I am however absolutely astonished at how bad the results of this challenge were. My friends have also been shocked – we all thought we had a much better chance at winning than this. This is either a huge disappointment or it confirms that we are in fact optimists and we still can dream of the 'what if...?'

The down side from this challenge is that I now receive lots of unsolicited e-mails even though I requested not to be contacted from companies. My suspicious side tends to wonder what happened to my competition entries where I requested no follow up or publicity material. But in case I continue to enter them forevermore I libel no one.

Postscript
I have recently been discussing my extreme bad luck with my competition entering with the husband of a pal who has been in the gambling and publishing businesses for many years. He was not in the least surprised at the return on my quantity of entries. He

explained how each entry would be calculated by the publishers or advertisers to be worth so much (I think he was talking about a figure of 5p or under). He made a rough calculation that for the amount of entries I made he would have expected a return of around £35 worth of prizes. So, higher than I actually got, but much, much, much lower than the glittering prizes and riches I had hoped for. So, back from cloud cuckoo land and back to reality for me then.

Chapter 24 - Revisiting October

Putting the thought back into Christmas

We did manage to save a fortune on this particular Xmas. Lots and lots of friends ended up receiving little bags of beautifully wrapped chocolate mint creams and in most cases this was, we think, a success. There were a few instances where we did not even try to pass this off as a present as we were sure they would go straight in the bucket and in those circumstances the would-be recipients received nothing!

Matt and my dad loved their photo books and painted mugs and cups. Daisy, surprisingly, was less keen on her expensive animatronics dog from her granddad (which went back to the shop as it was faulty) and instead loved, and continues to get great pleasure from her face paints, calendar and reward chart. We use the latter two on a daily basis. At the moment she needs another 10 stars to gain a day out (although we hardly keep her locked in a dungeon the rest of the month).

I have continued compiling the books for Oliver and Kitty and still record every major and minor event in the McGregor and Adams' households. This week I'll be adding the photos of them eating their first solids. If these books aren't best sellers, I don't know...

Will I be doing the same again next year, especially now that we do not have to worry so much about money? Possibly, but not likely. Without a doubt I will focus gift giving for my children mainly to things which they can 'do' and which they can spend hours and their imaginations using, but there will always be lots of the fun trinkets and stocking fillers which make it feel like Xmas. Matt and I have certainly learned a lot of lessons over the last year and a half, the greatest of which is that if we have our family and our health we do not really need any more 'stuff' and we have now changed our views to present buying accordingly. I can't get around the fact, however, that we didn't really succeed in this challenge. I'd argue that it is nigh on impossible to avoid the commercialism of Christmas unless you are going to avoid the festive season altogether and unless you do this for religious reasons, why on earth would anyone want to forgo Santa, sleigh bells, tinsel or twinkly lights?

Chapter 25 - Revisiting November

Gaining a skill

Update – still rubbish at making cakes. Still eating loads.

Chapter 26 - Revisiting December

Peace, goodwill and relaxation to all

My goodness – again I've been shedding a tear when reading about what was happening last year. It's amazing how quickly things can be forgotten and I've truly loved this chance to reflect on what's been happening in our lives.

As you are aware, our greatest little 'challenges' arrived, less than a month after our final experiment, ended. I never did get to watch any of the Audrey Hepburn DVDs. We are still unaware of why our roof was leaking. There's still a big hole cut in the bathroom ceiling. Now and again I wonder what the whirring or rustling noise is in the bathroom only to look up to see the polythene 'covering' the hole flapping about. Does it stress me out? Nah – I've got 4 other people in my household continually testing me on that front.

Chapter 27 – Epilogue

It's 10pm and I have just returned from my sanctuary, the spa I try to go to a couple of times a week. I lie in the hydro pool and relax – in my own way. The form this has taken over the last couple of weeks has been bouncing ideas around for a business I'm thinking of launching next summer – an internet based children's retail line. Whether this will actually pan out or just be another one of my many and varied schemes, is anyone's guess.

Essentially I believe I am a teacher and I totally love teaching but at the moment with 3 very young children and huge childcare costs I am constantly trying to think of other options which will afford me the opportunity to stay at home with the kids for as long as possible. Tonight I consciously stopped myself thinking about my next business and instead, so that I could start to tie up at lease one loose end, I sat down to try to put together this project in book form. Although I have worked in the book business in the past and know a little about publishing, I duly carted along the huge tome that is the 'Writer and Artists Yearbook' and began to read about how to prepare a manuscript to send to publishers. With this in mind I came home and started to talk to Matt about what I'm actually writing for the first time since the challenges began.

As you have probably been able to tell, Matt and I do not sing from the same hymn sheet. Indeed, when we met it was hardly a meeting of minds. Initially making contact with each other on the internet ("It's amazing what you can buy on E-bay," as my friend

Carol often says), a few months later we met in person for our 'blind date'. Matt turned up looking smart in his 'dressy' leather jacket and black silk shirt (can you hear me gag from the background?) and I arrived in my newly purchased bright pink furry coat, ala Wombles. Luckily we both thought the same of each other (not our types) and happily went our own ways but the friendship which had brought us together continued and over time we fell in love. The fact that on our second date Matt turned up with a bag of purchases he had just made at Waterstones and that these books were incredibly varied, from law books, to science fiction, historical novels and so on clinched the deal for me and when I later discovered that Matt was studying for a law degree so he would still be able to work when his eyesight deteriorated or went completely, I knew I had met a kindred spirit with drive and determination.

My own tendency to challenge myself I'm sure came from having a very entrepreneurial dad whose mind, although flighty, could be quite brilliant and/or mad at times. I grew up being encouraged to give everything a go and to this day I always give each new project my full commitment. Monetary gain has never been the deciding factor for me in defining whether projects have succeeded and in my dad's own book 'Easy Money' the dedication at the start says, "To my daughter, Jackie, who keeps trying to convince me a social conscience is more important than money. Her arguments become unstuck frequently, however, when the pub asks for hard cash, rather than a political diatribe, in exchange for gin and tonics!"

As well as Matty and my dad, the inspiration in my own life has come from friends and family who have been willing to 'have a go', whether it has been to travel adventurously, work selflessly to help others, start afresh in their domestic life leaving problem relationships behind and starting again with nothing or giving up lucrative careers to completely and bravely change direction later in life when job security should probably count greatly in their plans. Of course lately I've also been aware of the huge amount of respect parents and carers of children deserve, as this is so very often the most thankless profession. Last week I met another mum of twins, as well as a 2 and 3 year old, whose husband works away from home during the week. I salute her and I hope that this book can in a small way act as an inspiration or catalyst, even in a tiny way, to get others to think about how life could be changed for the better.

Don't think about copying my challenge ideas. There'd be no point. They are peculiar to my life and were things which I felt I needed to think about or work on. Instead ... good luck with yours.

Chapter 28

And then ......

After the epilogue .....

I know, I know ..... I should have structured the book better, but ......

Chapter 29 - November 2013

I did promise I'd bring you up to date.

As for the book – rejection, rejection, rejection. But .... some 'really good' rejections! In 2010 I sent off my manuscript to lots of different agents in the hope of finding representation. Very quickly, heavily filled, self-addressed envelopes containing my (read or unread) innermost thoughts crash-landed back on my doorstep. One or two crumbs were thrown my way in the process. A couple cited the economic climate or the lack of a known author 'name' as the reason for rejection and others suggested trying again at a later date or trying to drum up interest through a blog. Once I actually learned what a blog was, I quickly lost interest – learning how to produce one sounded to me akin to reading instruction manuals, so .... I carefully placed my manuscript in a drawer and continued with my more immediate calling of "Mummy", "Mum" or "Mama" depending on which of my children you speak to, housekeeper, friend and 'love of his life' to Matt (notice, I am not quoting here) and "Ms McGregor" to another couple of classrooms of enquiring (sometimes) minds!

Life continued on. Redundancy (or redeployment) again reared its ugly head for Matt. Did we panic? Did we lose sleep? Not really. We'd faced bigger challenges and could do so again. And would, for certain. That much we know.

But, did we have a happy ending?

We had another happy beginning. Married life began in May 2013. Unconventionally. Our lone wedding guests and witnesses were our mates Morag, Ben and Solomon. Little did they know that their acts of kindness during our desperate January challenge, of supplying us with bacon and egg rolls, would leave us eternally in their debt and strengthen our bonds of friendship forever – we salute you.

At our wedding meal our lovely Ollie tried to illustrate how we, as a family, try to tackle life ...

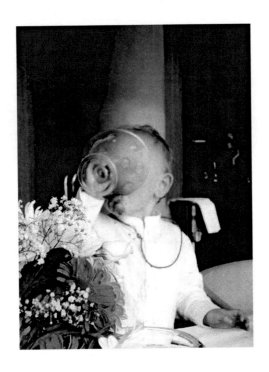

And so we face the future. I, for the first time in my life, am without my usual need to make the resolutions of stopping smoking and losing weight. The former battle was won many years ago, after breaking a 20 year habit and the latter finally clicked into place during the process of completing this book.

What? How? Why?

Because doing the challenges has truly taught me that ANYTHING is possible – and if you're reading this then I've just ticked another thing off my 'Bucket List'.

"Next!"

Lightning Source UK Ltd.
Milton Keynes UK
UKOW03f1828300114

225590UK00001B/9/P